Back Toward the Future

Books by the Author

Classical Evangelical Essays in Old Testament Interpretation (Editor)

The Old Testament in Contemporary Preaching

Toward an Old Testament Theology

Ecclesiastes: Total Life

Toward an Exegetical Theology: Biblical Exegesis for Preaching and Teaching

A Biblical Approach to Personal Suffering: Lamentations

Toward Old Testament Ethics

Malachi: God's Unchanging Love

The Uses of the Old Testament in the New

Quest for Renewal: Personal Revival in the Old Testament

Quality Living: Bible Studies in Ecclesiastes

A Tribute to Gleason Archer: Essays in Old Testament Studies (Co-editor)

Have You Seen the Power of God Lately? Studies in the Life of Elijah

Toward Rediscovering the Old Testament

Hard Sayings of the Old Testament

"Exodus" in *The Expositor's Bible Commentary*

Back Toward the Future

Hints for Interpreting Biblical Prophecy

Walter C. Kaiser, Jr.

BAKER BOOK HOUSE

Grand Rapids, Michigan 49516

© 1989 by Baker Book House Company
All rights reserved

Printed in the United States of America

Library of Congress Cataloging-in-Publication Data

Kaiser, Walter C.
    Back toward the future: hints for interpreting Biblical prophecy
    Walter C. Kaiser Jr.
        p.   cm.
    Includes bibliographies.
    ISBN 0-8010-5499-0
    1. Bible—Prophecies.   I. Title.
    BS647.2.K35   1989
    220.1'5—dc19   89-202
                                                                        CIP

to two special friends
who have

prayed for us,
laughed with us,
and encouraged us

Dr. Arthur and **Muriel Johnston**

Contents

Introduction

Mention prophecy and immediately the average person on the street conjures up images of seven-headed beasts, fire-spewing dragons, blood-red moons, falling stars, gigantic earthquakes, and unprecedented disasters. To be sure, prophecy has more than its share of exotica.

Suggest a Bible study in Daniel, Revelation, or one of the other books of the Bible that have a large section dealing with the future, and the response is quite predictable: "Oh, that? I think prophecy is too controversial, and I don't know of any two people who agree on what any of that 'stuff' means!"

You might think that the subject of horoscopes or signs of the zodiac had just been raised in an evangelical group of believers. But no. We are talking about part of God's revelation which otherwise is so revered and respected among us.

How did we ever become so gun-shy and timid on this subject?

Of course, there have been abuses—major abuses. But why should this intimidate us from a legitimate use and study of the biblical text on the same matters? That the subject matter and some of the literary forms may be a little different from the great narrative or didactic portions of Scripture with which we are most familiar is not an adequate reason for our abandoning this aspect of God's truth! How will we be able to defend ourselves before a holy God when he asks if we believed and taught "the whole counsel of God" (Acts 20:27 RSV)?

For every ten believers who are reluctant to study prophecy, there is one zealot whose love for the subject is exceeded only by a penchant for being cocksure about every identification he or she makes, including the date for every event slated for the future. In fact, we will not even need to press these zealots to tell us the exact date for the second coming of our Lord. Yes, they know that the Bible says that even our Lord did not know the time, but what they propose to tell us is not the "time," but only the week or the year! What can one say to such woodenheadedness? These are the people who give prophecy its bad press and who discourage others from its legitimate pursuit.

As soon as some of these frauds are exposed and the deadlines for some of their wildest predictions have passed, they leave in their wake an audience apathetic about making any careful exploration of the topic. The wild-eyed announcements that the western seaboard of California is going to fall off into the Pacific Ocean or that the Antichrist has already been born in some obscure town known only to a few select initiates are all too common and frequent. The shame of the matter is that many of these socalled prophecies are usually tied in with some Scripture or another. It's enough to make angels who attend church meetings (and I would assume Bible studies as well) weep.

In the meantime, a whole new generation grows up that has never been taught or exposed to the biblical pattern of thought on God's work in the future. Instead, that new generation becomes locked into the present and the past, but it has a very dim view of what is to come in the future. Little wonder, then, that they begin to develop shortsightedness and live only for themselves and for the present.

Are they totally responsible for the fact that they have been given no perspective concerning God's great work in the last days from which they can judge the value and worth of what they are presently doing?

Will our Lord be any less severe with us than he was with those two disciples on the road to Emmaus? Did he not roundly scold them for not knowing their scriptures about the events that were to come (Luke 24:25–27)? Are we any less foolish if we also neglect this area of study and leave large gaps in our thinking and acting?

In the providence of God, many of these matters tend to go in cycles. As soon as times start turning sour and the threat of an economic depression, an unstoppable plague, or involvement in another world war looms over the national spirit, all previous hesitations to enter into a study of the future are removed, and the topic returns with such a vengeance that one can hardly hear or think about anything else except predictions about the future.

Why must we wait until we are prodded by the disasters of history before we make a conscious and systematic effort to study all of the biblical books, including those that deal with this subject? It is our hope that we may all come to greater maturity in understanding and practicing the biblical approach to these matters. It will take some humility on our part to stand under all kinds of texts—including those that deal with prophecy—and let them inform, correct, rebuke, and make us wise to God's great climactic conclusion to history as he introduces the eternal state.

There is, of course, the slight matter of interpretation! "How," you protest, "can I be expected to study these portions of Scripture when I just cannot understand what in the world these biblical prophets are saying?"

That is where this little book of hints may come in handy. This little guide will not be a dull introduction to the subject. We will not subject the reader to a boring list of all the views and who has held what in the past. I can't

think of anything more dreadful. That is a quick way to
deter even the most undaunting soul. Besides, most of the
people we would bring up are now in heaven. And since
they no doubt already know how mistaken many of their
views were, it would needlessly embarrass them to have
their previous opinions dragged up again! (I assume that
many are part of that great cloud of witnesses mentioned
in Hebrews 12, who some feel are now observing us on
earth. It's possible, but not certain, that this is the correct
interpretation of that passage. I use the text more to tease
here than as an exegete.)

Neither shall we attempt to give a mini–Bible study on
each of the key prophetic passages of the Bible. There are
other places and types of books where that can be done.

Our aim is altogether different. We wish to take the fear
and dread of the unknown out of this subject for the
average reader of Scripture. While this book of hints
could be used as an introductory textbook for courses in
prophetic interpretation (whether in universities, Bible
colleges, seminaries, Bible-study groups, or the adult in-
structional program of the local church), our main focus
is the much larger reading audience of interested lay-
persons.

Many, indeed, have attempted to popularize this difficult subject, but very few of these efforts have suggested
a method for handling the whole topic. Instead, one is
usually treated to the conclusions of this or that interpreter. What has been needed all along is something
close to what Robert B. Girdlestone accomplished in 1901
in his delightful and most useful monograph, *The Grammar of Prophecy* (London: Eyre and Spottiswoode; Grand
Rapids: Kregel, 1955 reprint). At several points it will be
easy to detect my indebtedness to Girdlestone, but he
must not be held accountable for any garbling of his
views—especially since he too is no doubt in glory now
and would surely know the subject much better than I do
at present!

There remains only the pleasant task of thanking the Board of Directors of Trinity Evangelical Divinity School in Deerfield, Illinois, for providing a sabbatical from my regular duties and thereby allowing me, in the kindness also of our Lord, to complete this project along with several others. My heartful thanks to our God for a most enlightened board, which has offered over the past twenty years one of the most generous sabbatical plans I know of. This has made it possible for a host of scholarly and popular works to extend around the world the ministry we at Trinity Evangelical Divinity School have for Christ.

I must not forget to mention my wife, Margaret Ruth, for her patience while I was occupied with writing *Back Toward the Future*. She picked up my share of many routine tasks in life, thus freeing me for concentrating on this task.

My prayer is that each reader who picks up this volume might be encouraged to enter for the first time (or belatedly to reenter) the wonderfully fascinating, but equally challenging and helpful waters of biblical prophecy. The subject matter is too important for us to neglect it; indeed, the Scriptures have so much to say in this regard that those who neglect it cannot be considered truly biblical and obedient to the whole counsel of God. It is high time we were involved in this area along with all the rest of scriptural truth.

PART 1

Hermeneutics

1

Make Prophetic Interpretation Center on the Living God

Everyone is more than a little curious about the future. But where can a person go to find out about the future? Surely it is a denial of God and his revelation to try to gain such information by consulting horoscopes or people who profess to have contact with the spirit world. Yet that is exactly what is being advocated in our complex and spiritually starved world. Why, even the wife of the president of the United States in this twentieth century admits to using such sources in order to determine when events should be timed so as to be under the most auspicious signs of the planets and stars!

But why do our contemporaries avoid going to Scripture for such help? There they would find a full array of predictions spread over many centuries from the pens of many writers, but exhibiting a unity and pattern unrivaled anywhere else. The Scripture's focus is never on the isolated act or event in itself, but on the eternal God who spoke all these utterances and who has been overseeing history as it moves to the conclusion that he has eternally planned for it.

In fact, prediction is so natural to and so much a part

of the divine activity that it can almost be ascribed as an attribute of God himself. One evidence of this is the comparison implied in God's challenge through Isaiah the prophet to the dead idols of the nations:

> Bring in your idols to tell us what is going to happen. Tell us what the former things were, so that we may consider them and know their final outcome. Or declare to us the things to come, tell us what the future holds, so we may know that you are gods. Do something, whether good or bad, so that we will be dismayed and filled with fear. [Isa. 41:22–23]

Many other evidences can be cited; for instance,

> Who foretold this long ago, who declared it from the distant past? Was it not I, the LORD? And there is no God apart from me, a righteous God and a Savior; there is none but me. [Isa. 45:21b–c]

> I am God, and there is no other; I am God, and there is none like me. I make known the end from the beginning, from ancient times, what is still to come. I say: My purpose will stand, and I will do all that I please. [Isa. 46:9b–10]

> Surely the Sovereign LORD does nothing without revealing his plan to his servants the prophets. [Amos 3:7]

Biblical prophecies, then, are neither lucky guesses nor wholesale forgeries. They must be read thoughtfully and related to the larger scheme of revelation. Prediction is not just an additive to the rest of revelation—it is one of the methods of revelation!

It is particularly through God the Son that the prophecies of the Old and New Testament come into their sharpest focus. That is the summation given in Revelation 19:10—"For the testimony of Jesus is the spirit of prophecy." Thus the main line of witness of the Old Testament was to the Messiah, Jesus of Nazareth. All prophecies, whether central or subsidiary to this theme, contributed to it in one way or another.

Likewise, the focus of New Testament prophecy is the coming of Messiah, both past and future. The words "the testimony of Jesus is the spirit of prophecy" have been taken in two different ways: either Jesus is the common theme or substance of all prophecy, or the true spirit of prophecy always manifests itself in bearing witness to Jesus. The former interpretation seems to be preferred, for most who take the second option usually end up writing off this part of the verse as an unnecessary gloss (addition by a translator) by someone who had Revelation 22:8–9 in mind. Both views, however, stress the centrality of Jesus for prophecy.

If the Messiah is the central focus of prophecy, what are the general characteristics of most biblical prophecies? In the stately judgment of Robert B. Girdlestone there are six characteristics:

1. Biblical prophecy plainly foretells things to come without clothing them in ambiguities such as the oracles of the pagan nations.
2. It entails designed and intended predictions rather than unwitting prophecies or "lucky guesses" that just happened to come to pass.
3. It is written, published, or proclaimed prior to the event it refers to and could not have been foreseen by ordinary human ingenuity.
4. It is subsequently fulfilled in accordance with the words of the original prediction. (This will be evident, provided due regard is given to the laws of prophetic speech and interpretation.)
5. Prophecy does not work out its own fulfilment, but it stands as a witness until after the event has taken place.
6. A biblical prophecy is not an isolated prediction, but it can be correlated with other prophecies and as such is one of a long series of predictions.[1]

1. Robert B. Girdlestone, *The Grammar of Prophecy: A Systematic Guide to Biblical Prophecy* (Grand Rapids: Kregel, 1955), p. 1.

There are a few prophecies that do not fit every category given here. Where these exceptions exist, however, they do not cancel out the thrust and the spirit of the six characteristics.

The number of prophecies in the Bible is so large and their distribution so evenly spread through both Testaments and all types of literary forms that the interpreter is alerted to the fact that he or she is dealing with a major component of the Bible. According to the calculations of J. Barton Payne, there are 8,352 verses (out of a total for the whole Bible of 31,124) with predictive material in them.[2] This means that 27 percent of the Bible deals with prophecy! Payne calculated that out of the Old Testament's 23,210 verses, 6,641 (or 28.5 percent) contain predictive material, while 1,711 verses of the New Testament's 7,914 (or 21.5 percent) include predictive material. These verses discuss 737 separate prophetic topics.

The only books that have no predictions, Payne asserted, are Ruth and Song of Solomon in the Old Testament and Philemon and 3 John in the New Testament. The remaining sixty-two books all have some representation. Table 1 lists the three Old Testament and three New Testament books with the greatest number of pro-

Table 1 **Biblical Books High in Predictive Material**

	Total Verses of Prophecy	Percentage of Predictive Material
Old Testament		
Ezekiel	821	65
Jeremiah	812	60
Isaiah	754	59
New Testament		
Matthew	278	26
Revelation	256	63
Luke	250	22

2. J. Barton Payne, *Encyclopedia of Biblical Prophecy: The Complete Guide to Scriptural Predictions and Their Fulfillment* (New York: Harper and Row, 1973), pp. 631–82.

phetic verses. The highest percentages of predictive material are found in the small books of Zephaniah (89 percent), Obadiah (81 percent), and Nahum (74 percent). In the New Testament, the honors go to Revelation (63 percent), Hebrews (45 percent), and 2 Peter (41 percent).

Thus it can be seen that prophecy must not be passed off lightly or regarded as a matter of indifference. It comes close to involving almost a third of the biblical message! This in itself ought to be more than enough reason for us to get on with our study of this neglected area of the Scriptures, or we too will earn the scornful remark made about the generation of our Lord: they knew how to discern the signs in the sky in order to predict the weather, but they had no discernment or knowledge about how to judge the signs of the time (Luke 12:54–56).

Prophecy, as we are using the term here, is not the same thing as forecasting the weather or "predicting" where the futures market or stock market is headed in the next few months. Only God possesses the requisite knowledge of the future which allows him to "declare to us the things to come, [and to] tell us what the future holds" (Isa. 41:22–23). Therefore we shall define prophecy as "a miracle of knowledge, a declaration or representation of something future, beyond human sagacity to discern or to calculate."[3] God disclosed his secrets to his sons and daughters through his apostles and prophets.

So strong was this linkage of prediction with the prophets that they used to be called "seers" (1 Sam. 9:9). A person who wanted to know something that could not be learned by ordinary investigation would instinctively turn to a seer. Consider the case of Saul's servant, who turned to Samuel because "everything he says comes true" (1 Sam. 9:6).

In a similar manner, Jesus said, "See, I have told you

ahead of time" (Matt. 24:25). In another passage which is even more striking our Lord affirmed, "I am telling you now before it happens, so that when it does happen you will believe that I am He" (John 13:19). This passage teaches us two things about prediction: (1) historical fulfilment is the ultimate interpreter of prophecy, for it is only when it comes to pass that we will know with certainty what that prophecy really meant (a caution for humility in this area); and (2) all fulfilment of prophecy vindicates the one who is the great "I am." It never proves that we were right or that our charts were more accurate than someone else's; on the contrary, it proves that only God knows the future, and that only he spoke the truth before it came into being.

If it be doubted that the subject matter of prophecy is pure prediction, the thought could not be more succinctly and definitely stated than it is in Isaiah 42:9: "new things I declare; before they spring into being I announce them to you." Modern scholarship, however, has steadfastly resisted the concept that Scripture includes prediction. In order to circumvent this claim, moderns sadly invent the thesis that all these so-called prophecies were written after the fact; that is, in order to keep the attention of their listeners and readers, the prophets had the habit of describing events as if they were predicting them in advance, when in truth they were reporting those events only after they had happened! Of course from our perspective (and, I might add, from God's point of view also), there is no evidence for this massive charge of what amounts to fraud. It is merely the philosophical prejudices of our contemporaries against the facts that God can make himself known in speech and that he can reveal the future. But as one of their own peers wrote, "Whether modern scholars like it or not [and they don't], prediction was the way the N[ew] T[estament] writers themselves related the testament."[4]

4. Raymond E. Brown et al., eds., 2 vols., *The Jerome Biblical Commentary* (Englewood Cliffs, N.J.: Prentice-Hall, 1968), vol. 2, p. 615.

Another way of disparaging the biblical predictions is by emphasizing that the New Testament fulfilments are superior to and diverge immensely from what the Old Testament writers had intended or known. But to glorify the fulfilment at the expense of the prediction is to disparage testimony to the greatness of the living God. Every miracle of God, whether in word or deed, had as its object what Joshua and the people of Israel realized when the waters of Jordan rolled back, "This is how you will know that the living God is among you" (Josh. 3:10). Equally relevant was the word spoken by the Holy Spirit through Ezekiel, "When all this comes true—and it surely will—then they will know that a prophet has been among them" (Ezek. 33:33).

Often God would use the fulfilment of the short-range predictions (e.g., the ripping open of the altar of King Jeroboam in 1 Kings 13:3) as the basis for validating the longer-range predictions which awaited many years for their fulfilment (e.g., in the same passage [v. 2] the coming of King Josiah is predicted, a prophecy which was fulfilled three hundred years later).

Of course the subject matter to which each prediction contributes extends way beyond any single prediction on that topic, but this is no cause for interpreters to jump to the conclusion that biblical prophecies revealed to the prophets extended so far beyond their human consciousnesses that they were often left scratching their heads over just what it was that they themselves meant by their own prophecies! True, 1 Peter 1:10–12 does depict the prophets as baffled. "[They] searched intently and with the greatest care," but their search was not for the truth-intention of what they had written. Instead, it was for "the time and circumstances to which the Spirit of Christ in them was pointing when he predicted the sufferings of Christ and the glories that would follow. It was revealed to them that they were not serving themselves, but you," declared Peter. Therefore, we may be certain that the prophets' area of ignorance about their own prophecies existed exactly where our ignorance occurs: *the time* of Christ's coming.

That is the only issue for which they searched and in-
quired diligently—even as we do. However, if the prophets
were short in this one area, they were certain in five other
areas. They knew for sure that they were announcing (1)
the Messiah, (2) Messiah's sufferings, (3) Messiah's coming
in glorious splendor to rule and reign, (4) the sequence of
those two events—suffering first and then glory, and (5) a
message that had relevance not only for the Old Testament
saint, but for another day as well, relevance which Peter
declares extends to those of us in the church.

It is morally wrong to take a descriptive passage such
as Caiaphas's inadvertent prophecy in John 11:49–52 and
turn it into a normative passage which proves that the
prophets often "spoke better than they knew" (a saying
which, by the way, is not a biblical quotation, even though
I have heard it so frequently cited in our circles one would
think that it is). On those occasions where the prophet
confesses ignorance of his own visions (Dan. 8:27; 12:8;
Zech. 4:13), either they involve the question of time or he
has attempted to understand what is being said before he
writes it down. Revelation as revelation never circumvents
the understanding of the writer, as if it were a cryptic
mystery code which can be interpreted on several levels
by several different decipherers, depending on their grasp of
certain esoteric inductions into the subsequent values of
the symbols or words. Scripture does not affirm that there
were uncertainties in the minds of the prophets about
what they wrote; in fact, 1 Peter 1:10–12 asserts the reverse. Neither can we find concrete examples of predictions where God's originally intended meaning was missed
by the writer to whom it was given. The meaning given to
the prophets represents in its fulness the meaning of the
Holy Spirit, even though that meaning may be only a part
of the total subject to which it contributes and only one
of many avenues through which the text in question may
be applied.

Thus, to glorify the fulfilment at the expense of the

prediction is to demean the presence of the living God in his word. But it is equally wrong to do the reverse. To glorify the prediction at the expense of the fulfilment is to miss the significance of the gospel of our Lord Jesus Christ. For it is through the fulfilment that we come to know that the one who has spoken was none other than our Lord himself. Both sides of the prediction must be upheld: the predictive word and the fulfilling event.

The prophetic word must not be viewed as existing in a vacuum. Prophecy and providence run together. God's prophetic word was usually spoken into a historical situation. So closely is history tied to the prophetic word that it is often hard to disentangle them. God has deliberately put these utterances into the stream of history so that we might know that both the word and history belong to him. Furthermore, this serves to insure that the utterance will not be taken as an isolated word without correlation to what God has said or done in the past or present. Thus, the promises to Abraham, Isaac, and Jacob are repeated over and over again in the midst of a host of very complicated everyday affairs. They are located in space and time, and forward movement is realized, since what was promised then continues directly to affect every Christian to this very day.

The Greek oracles, on the other hand, did precisely the opposite. They would utter their "prophecies" in such a way as to make sure that they had no connection with either space or time. Since the Greeks were anxious to escape both this world and time itself in order to be joined to a nebulous spirit-world, they naturally had little concern for either of these realities. Scripture dared to put God's prophetic word right in the midst of both space and time.

Not only was prophecy tied to history, it was also closely related to the realm of the practical and spiritual. Seldom, if ever, was it the purpose of God to surprise, to shock, or merely to excite fascination with the future. Nor was prophecy in any sense a therapeutic tranquilizer to be used as a substitute for appropriate action in the Christian life.

Sadly, some have become so enthralled with studying prophecy that they are of no earthly good to their Lord, others, and themselves. In their distorted view, things are continuing to get worse and worse, and all of this is nothing less than a sign that the coming of the Lord is near. Accordingly, the coming of the Lord becomes an excuse for avoiding meaningful involvement in the daily tasks of faithful living before God. In two separate letters Paul had to remind the Thessalonians not to get so carried away with the doctrine of the coming of the Lord as to drop all work and become idle (1 Thess. 5:14; 2 Thess. 3:6). That same danger remains to the present day. Some, trying to outguess our Lord, have concluded that any long-range planning is useless, as is any task which lays on us a concern for something beyond the present moment.

Scripture does not allow for a fatalistic spirit which says in effect, "Whatever God wants to happen will happen; I'm just waiting for the coming of the Lord." On the contrary, every prediction about the future is simultaneously a call for action. The predictive elements, then, are generally subservient to the practical and spiritual claims that our Lord has laid on our lives.

Witness, for instance, the way David acted when he was given the prophecy that Saul would come down to the town of Keilah where he was staying and that the citizens of Keilah, whom David had just delivered from the Philistines, would hand him over to Saul (1 Sam. 23:10–12). Knowing the certainty of the prediction did not reduce David to immobility; instead, he fled the city! Therefore, the certainty of prophecy is no excuse for our not acting, as if God's providence required no further involvement from us.

In almost every context where a prophecy is recorded, there is usually some injunction, command, or word urging us on to holy living and acting. Thus, after Paul has concluded the great teaching on the resurrection of Jesus Christ (1 Cor. 15), there immediately follows an injunction equivalent to "Will the ushers please come forward to take up the offering" (16:1–3). Likewise, the apostle Peter urges us, "Be holy in all you do," after he has announced the grace to be given us when Jesus Christ is revealed (1 Pet. 1:13–16).

The prophet Micah's proclamation that "because of you [sinners], Zion will be plowed like a field, Jerusalem will become a heap of rubble, the temple hill a mound overgrown with thickets" (Mic. 3:12), produced a definite effect on the people who heard him in the mid-700s B.C. We know this from a reference in Jeremiah a century later (Jer. 26:17–19). Micah's preaching had produced the effect of repentance and the fear of the Lord. And since the people of that day repented and sought the Lord, the Lord, in turn, repented of the evil that he had threatened to bring on the people. The prophecy had had its effect in the areas of confession of sin, avoidance of evil, and obedience seen in good works. That is precisely what God wants to happen to us through our study of prophecy. Our being highly informed about the future will serve little good if it does not simultaneously result in a whole different orientation of our lives and our actions. Prophecy is not a sterile, remote subject which has an interesting trivia list. It is a call to action based on the certainty of the future acts of God in space and time. It is a call to repentance based on the present drift of an evil society and a backsliding church. It is a call to faith and belief in the living God who is doing all things well after the counsel of his own wise and holy will.

For Further Study

Beecher, Willis J. *The Prophets and the Promise,* esp. chaps. 8, 16. New York: Crowell, 1905; Grand Rapids: Baker, 1963.

Clouse, Robert G. "The Danger of Mistaken Hopes." In *Dreams, Vi-*

sions and Oracles: The Layman's Guide to Biblical Prophecy, ed.
Carl E. Armerding and W. Ward Gasque, pp. 27–39. Grand Rapids:
Baker, 1977.

Girdlestone, Robert B. *The Grammar of Prophecy: A Systematic Guide
to Biblical Prophecy,* chaps. 1–2. Grand Rapids: Kregel, 1955.

Green, Joel B. *How to Read Prophecy,* chaps. 1–4. Downers Grove,
Ill.: Inter-Varsity, 1984.

Payne, J. Barton. *Encyclopedia of Biblical Prophecy: The Complete
Guide to Scriptural Predictions and Their Fulfillment,* pp. 3–150.
New York: Harper and Row, 1973; Grand Rapids: Baker, 1980.

2

Don't Believe Everything Everyone Says About the Future

It's all too easy to make predictions; it's much more difficult to supply criteria or tests which, prior to fulfilment or nonfulfilment, can determine whether those predictions or prophecies are true or false. There are predictions about who will win a given election, which team will have a winning season and take the championship, and where the economy is headed in the future. It is difficult to evaluate such predictions. The question arises: Are we just as helpless in assessing the predictions in the Bible as we are those which we encounter in everyday life?

Our Lord warned that we should "watch out for false prophets" (Matt. 7:15). There were and there continue to be fakes and charlatans. However, even though prophecy can be faked, our Lord also warned that we should "not treat prophecies with contempt" (1 Thess. 5:20). Instead, Paul advised, "Test everything. Hold on to the good. Avoid every kind of evil" (vv. 21–22).

Apparently it is possible to distinguish between true and false prophecy. Nevertheless, it is difficult. Jesus alerted us to the fact that false prophets come "in sheep's clothing,

but inwardly they are ferocious wolves" (Matt. 7:15).
Therefore, it will be necessary that we develop extremely
sensitive biblical consciences if we are going to be able to
detect these frauds.

False prophets can be sent to try our faith and to see if
we are really depending solely on the living God. But they
carry with them marked characteristics. Jeremiah 23 ex-
poses four such telltale signs found in these lying, false
prophets.

First of all, the false prophets can be detected by their
immoral lifestyles: "They prophesied by Baal and led my
people Israel astray. . . . They commit adultery and live a
lie" (vv. 13–14). Hence the source of their words is not
God, but some dead idol or the evil and satanic realm
itself. Their lives are astonishing lies which violate the
laws of God as if they were a privileged class.

A second characteristic is the fact that false prophets
are crowd pleasers. If the people want to hear, "Peace,
peace," they will be sure to acquiesce and to say what will
grant them favor in the eyes of the masses. In Jeremiah's
day they filled the people "with false hopes [and spoke]
visions from their own minds, not from the mouth of the
LORD" (v. 16). They kept insisting, "You will have peace"
(v. 17).

Micah, another prophet of the Lord, agreed: "As for the
prophets who lead my people astray, if one feeds them,
they proclaim 'peace'; if he does not, they prepare to wage
war against him" (Mic. 3:5). Clearly the message is dependent on the disposition of the listeners. What is said is not
determined by the will of God; it is conditioned by what
people give or fail to give the prophet. False prophets are
like after-dinner speakers who know how to humor their
audience. But they know nothing about the word of God
or how serious it is to fall into the hands of an angry God.

In addition to their moral failures and their seeking pop-
ularity, false prophets fail to distinguish their own thoughts
from God's revelation. Jeremiah condemned this practice:

" 'For what has straw to do with grain?' declares the LORD. 'Is not my word like fire,' declares the LORD, 'and like a hammer that breaks a rock in pieces?' " (23:28–29). How dare these religious buffoons claim, "This is the oracle of the LORD" (v. 34), or say, "I had a dream! I had a dream!" (v. 25)? These lying prophets "prophesy the delusions of their own minds" (v. 26). Such substitution of a human word for the divine word is unconscionable.

Closely related to this negative criterion is a fourth: plagiarism. These rascals steal God's true words and use them to their own ends. They "distort the words of the living God" (v. 36) and lead God's people astray with their mendacious claptrap (v. 32). But the Lord says that he is "against the prophets who steal from one another words supposedly from me" (v. 30). Such repeating of one another's words and such stealing from God and quoting out of context amount to nothing but "reckless lies" (v. 32). The picture is not a pretty one at all. The dreams, visions, and words out of one's own mind and heart must be sharply distinguished from the words, visions, and dreams that come from God. So overpowering is the real thing that Jeremiah felt as if he had been shaken in all his bones (v. 9). He had to say what God wanted him to say even if he did not feel it would be particularly popular or chic for him to do so.

The conflict between the true and false prophet can be seen in the account of the four hundred prophets of Ahab versus the prophet Micaiah son of Imlah in 1 Kings 22. Micaiah was summoned to advise concerning the plan to go to war against Ramoth Gilead, even though he had previously issued unpopular verdicts from God to Ahab and Jezebel. Micaiah opposed the unanimous verdict of the four hundred prophets, charging that they had been the targets of a "lying spirit" that had gone out by the permission of God to deceive those who had so willfully given themselves over to speak what was wrong and not in accord with the word of God (vv. 21–23). Zedekiah, one of the four hundred, feeling the rebuke sharply, walked up to Micaiah, slapped his face, and sneered, "Which way did the spirit from the LORD go when he went from me to speak to you?" (v. 24). The false prophets in this episode laid claim to speaking by the Spirit of God, but that did not make it so. Their predictions did not come true; only Micaiah's word happened.

The Micaiah episode was not an isolated incident in Israel's history. In Jeremiah 28, Jeremiah faced stiff competition from a certain Hananiah. In a very embarrassing confrontation in a public place, Hananiah not only broke the wooden yoke which God had told Jeremiah to wear around his neck, but also gave a word from the Lord which differed from Jeremiah's. Hananiah even dared to use the prophetic formula, "This is what the LORD says." Hananiah's word was that the Babylonian yoke would be removed shortly and that within two years the temple vessels taken when Jerusalem fell would be returned (28:2–3).

God's rejoinder to this impudent act was to tell Jeremiah to make and wear an iron yoke. Furthermore, Hananiah was to be told, "The LORD has not sent you, yet you have persuaded this nation to trust in lies. Therefore, this is what the LORD says, 'I am about to remove you from the face of the earth. This very year you are going to die, because you have preached rebellion against the LORD'" (28:15–16). Less than two months later Hananiah died (28:17; cf. 28:1)!

Both of these narratives supply us with more than mere illustrations. Indeed, they exemplify, in part, the five tests for a prophet recorded in Deuteronomy 13:1–5 and 18:14–22:

1. Membership in Israel (18:18)
2. Speaking in the name of the Lord (18:19)
3. Predictions of the near and distant future (18:22)
4. Performance of signs and wonders (13:1–2)
5. Conformity with previous revelation (13:2–5)

Israel's advantage over the other nations was that she had "been entrusted with the very words of God" (Rom. 3:1–2). With the exception of Balaam (Num. 22), who only tends to prove the rule, all the biblical prophets came from Jewish roots. That was a unique privilege conferred on Israel by the living God.

The second test to ferret out impostors was the test of speaking in the name of the Lord. To presume to pronounce something in the name of the living God involved an awesome claim. Obviously, this test, unlike the other four, was sufficient in and of itself to indicate genuineness. The problem here is that there were those who were impudent enough to prophesy falsely in God's name.

Another notorious case, besides the one of Hananiah, was that strange incident involving the man of God from Judah in 1 Kings 13. Although he, as God's prophet, had been forewarned by God not to tarry or eat in Bethel after he had delivered the word from God, he was deceived by the lying words of an old prophet in Bethel who claimed to speak in the name of the Lord. The old man coaxed, " 'I too am a prophet, as you are. And an angel said to me by the word of the LORD: "Bring him back with you to your house so that he may eat bread and drink water." ' (But he was lying to him)" (1 Kings 13:18).

Unfortunately, the man from Judah acquiesced (in spite of God's clear warnings). It happened that while they were seated at the table a true word came from God to the old prophet who had lied! Once again the old prophet claimed to speak in the name of the Lord (and this time he was telling the truth), "This is what the LORD says: 'You have defied the word of the LORD and have not kept the command the LORD your God gave you. . . . Therefore your body will not be buried in the tomb of your fathers' " (1 Kings 13:21–22). And that is what happened: while on his way home the man of God from Judah was killed by a lion. So here is the case of an authentic prophet's being deceived by the words of another who claimed to be speaking in the name of the Lord. The problem was that the man of God from Judah forgot that the words of a prophet must agree with what God has previously revealed. The five tests are interconnected.

The actual fulfilment of a prophecy was the third test for the truth of a prophet's claim. Some prophecies were too far in the future for any contemporary audience to know if the words were true or not. That is why fulfilment of a prophet's words regarding the immediate or near future became the basis for trusting what he said about the distant future. This is plainly illustrated in the case of Hananiah and Jeremiah. Surely the people were impressed when this false prophet, after making a public fuss to embarrass Jeremiah, suddenly died. That should have been enough to persuade most of them, but many, then as now, probably just passed it off as a lucky guess. Likewise, when King Ahab's body was brought back from the battle at Ramoth Gilead, in accordance with Micaiah's grim prediction, the insolent four hundred should have been utterly disgraced. Alas, they survived, as does most evil for the time being.

Often God authenticated his word about the future by accompanying signs and wonders, as our fourth test leads us to expect. Samuel's words were validated by the miracle of the thunder and rain (1 Sam. 12:16–18). Moses' words to Pharaoh were backed up by preliminary signs and then by the miracles of the ten plagues (Exod. 4:1–9, 21). And so it was for Elijah, Elisha, and numerous other prophets. Of course the false prophets were able to replicate many of these signs and wonders. Since the contest was a supernatural one, it is easy to understand that some were granted limited powers by Satan to produce their own miracles in order to mislead the believing community if they could.

Finally, the message of the prophet had to be in harmony with all the previous revelation of God. What God has said in the light, no one ever has the right to doubt in the darkness—or at any other time. The prophet from Judah could have saved himself from a lot of trouble had he remembered this in 1 Kings 13. God will never contradict himself; his revelation will always agree with what he has said previously.

Some will object, "But what about all those prophecies in Scripture that were not fulfilled?" It became popular in the nineteenth century to point to the following as examples of prophecies that were not fulfilled in precisely the manner that had been predicted:

1. The prophecy of the ruin of Tyre by Nebuchadnezzar (Ezek. 26:7–14; 29:17–20)
2. Jonah's prophecy of the destruction of Nineveh (Jon. 3:4)
3. Elijah's prophecy against King Ahab for murdering Naboth (1 Kings 21:17–29)
4. Isaiah's prophecy on the destruction of Damascus (Isa. 17:1)

Of course what is overlooked are the hundreds of prophecies that have been accurately fulfilled. Attention has been focused on these four because many critics have failed either to read the text carefully or to be aware of certain other features such as an understood "unless you repent."

The so-called nonfulfilment of prophecies is to be explained on the basis of the threefold classification of biblical prophecy; that is, prophecy may be *unconditionally* fulfilled, *conditionally* fulfilled, or *sequentially* fulfilled. All three types are commonly used and are accompanied by indicators that aid the reader and interpreter in distinguishing between the three types of prophecies.

Those prophecies in which God obligated himself to carry out the terms for the fulfilment are called unconditional. No obligation rests on any mortal, past or present, for their realization. God has bound himself to see to it that these prophecies are carried out; therefore, there is

no shadow of doubt or tentativeness as to whether they
will come to fruition or not.

The list of such unconditional prophecies is not long,
but they are indeed as central, in most respects, for our
salvation as one can get. They include God's covenant
with the seasons (Gen. 8:21–22), God's promise to Abraham (Gen. 12:2–3; 15:9–21), God's promise to David
(2 Sam. 7:8–16), God's promise of the new covenant (Jer.
31:31–34), and God's promise of the new heavens and the
new earth (Isa. 65:17–19; 66:22–24). As Genesis 15:17 so
graphically describes it, only God (depicted as the fiery
presence) moved between the pieces Abraham had set up.
In effect, God said as he moved between the animals that
had been split in half, "May what has happened to these
animals happen to me if I do not fulfil the terms of this
prediction!" This is what it means "to make a covenant"
or, more literally, "to cut a covenant." Had this been a
bilateral covenant, Abraham would also have been asked
to move between the pieces and to obligate himself with
the same oath of malediction and death in the event he
failed to keep the terms of the covenant. However, in this
case any action on Abraham's part was unnecessary since
God had taken the full responsibility on himself. Nothing
depended on man or on any circumstances for fulfilment
of the covenant; it all depended on God alone.

The majority of the prophecies in the Old Testament,
however, were of the conditional type. The great teaching
texts that they rested on were Leviticus 26 and Deuteronomy 28. These two texts with their alternative prospects for obedience and disobedience were directly quoted
or alluded to by the sixteen writing prophets literally
hundreds of times. This phenomenon is so important that
we have reserved a whole chapter for its discussion
(chap. 5).

What should be said here is that almost every prophecy,
except for those involved with the provision of our salvation and with the creation, maintenance, and renewal
of the universe, has an "unless" or "if" (either expressed

or understood) connected with it. That is the import of the message of Leviticus 26 and Deuteronomy 28.

Of the four most commonly pressed examples of non-fulfilled prophecies mentioned above, Jonah's prophecy of the destruction of Nineveh fits squarely into this category. Even though neither Jonah nor God mentioned any conditions with regard to the threatened judgment in forty days, both Jonah and the people of Nineveh were aware that such was the case. This explains Jonah's terrible reluctance to even announce this severe disaster upon his most despised enemies; he rightly feared that if the king and people of Nineveh once moved toward repentance for the sins that occasioned the decision of God, the threatened judgment would be averted and postponed. Such is the nature of conditional prophecy.

A number of prophecies do not comfortably fit in either the unconditional or the conditional category. Those prophecies are sequentially fulfilled and thus are a subspecies of the conditional type. The prophecy of Ezekiel 26:7–14 falls into this third category:

> For this is what the Sovereign LORD says: From the north I am going to bring against Tyre Nebuchadnezzar king of Babylon. . . . He will ravage your settlements on the mainland . . . he will set up siege works against you. . . . He will direct the blows of his battering rams against your walls and demolish your towers with his weapons. His horses will be so many that they will cover you with dust. . . . He will kill your people with the sword, and your strong pillars will fall to the ground. They will plunder your wealth and loot your merchandise; they will break down your walls and demolish your fine houses and throw your stones, timber and rubble into the sea. . . .

According to many critics of biblical prophecy, Ezekiel in 29:18–20 admits the nonfulfilment of this prophecy:

> Son of man, Nebuchadnezzar king of Babylon drove his army in a hard campaign against Tyre. . . . Yet he and his

army got no reward from the campaign he led against
Tyre. . . . I have given him Egypt as a reward for his efforts
because he and his army did it for me, declares the Sovereign LORD.

But is this an example of nonfulfilment? Ezekiel 26:12
does not promise Nebuchadnezzar that he would profit
from his invasion of Tyre. Neither does history relate anything which would refute the fact that the mainland city
of Tyre was indeed conquered by this Babylonian king.
The crucial point that has gone unobserved is that Ezekiel
shifts his pronouns in the middle of his prophecy. In verse
12 he suddenly switches to the third-person-plural pro-
noun "they."

This switch is an important interpretive clue to both
the original audience and us that Nebuchadnezzar would
not carry out all that is prophesied here. There is a sequence in the complete fulfilment of this word against
Tyre. Nebuchadnezzar took the mainland city of Tyre after
a long siege. But it was Alexander the Great, more than
two hundred years later, to whom the total conquest would
be granted. Indeed, Alexander literally scrapped the remains of the previously destroyed mainland city of Tyre
and threw the "stones, timber and rubble into the sea"
(26:12). With this material he built a causeway one-half
mile out into the Mediterranean Sea in order to dislodge
from their island home the Tyrians who had escaped Nebuchadnezzar's conquest of their mainland city in the 570s
B.C. Alexander, then, in the 330s completed the sequence
that had been tied together in Ezekiel's single prophecy.

In like manner, Elijah's prophecy about King Ahab's
punishment for the murder of Naboth is fulfilled in a sequence of acts. To be sure, the text is most emphatic: "Say
to him, 'This is what the LORD says: Have you not mur-
dered a man and seized his property?' Then say to him,
'This is what the LORD says: In the place where dogs licked
up Naboth's blood, dogs will lick up your blood—yes,

yours!' " (1 Kings 21:19). However, since Ahab humbled himself when he heard this devastating prophecy ("Have you noticed how Ahab has humbled himself before me? Because he has humbled himself, I will not bring this disaster in his day, but I will bring it on his house in the days of his son"—1 Kings 21:29), the threat was not carried out on Ahab. In accordance with the principle of conditional prophecy and the compassion of our God, Ahab was spared from having his blood licked up in the very spot where he had wrongfully spilled Naboth's blood outside of Jezreel. Instead, the dogs licked up Ahab's blood in Samaria when the chariot in which he had died in battle was being washed (1 Kings 22:38). The critics fail to notice that the threatened doom was carried out against his son a decade later, for there was no repentance on the part of his son Joram. Joram's corpse was cast onto Naboth's ground (2 Kings 9:25–26). Once again we have an example of a sequential prophecy within the category of conditional prediction.

Isaiah 17:1 was also raised as an example of a nonfulfilled prophecy. But this complaint fails to note that Damascus stands here for the whole Syrian nation of which it is the capital. Furthermore, there is a play on the similar-sounding Hebrew words of "city" and "ruin" (mēʿîr and mĕʿî). Of course the city of Damascus exists today, but it does not exert the power and influence that it wielded prior to its fall in 732 B.C. Further, a careful reading will reveal that the prophet did not indicate that Damascus was facing a permanent destruction and full eradication of its existence from off the face of the earth.

These, then, are the various ways in which the prophetic sections of the Bible can be fulfilled. Readers of that day were to be on guard against anyone who falsely claimed to speak a word from God. There were fakes, but they could be detected by their telltale characteristics. And there were tests for a true prophet, which are basically the same tests we use today.

Certainly there is no reason why we should believe everything everyone says about the future. What God says about the future, however, is of more than just passing interest to all who know the Savior and who revere his word.

For Further Study

Manahan, Ronald E. "A Theology of Pseudoprophets: A Study of Jeremiah." *Grace Theological Journal* 1 (1980): 77–96.

Renner, J. T. E. "False and True Prophets." *Reformed Theological Review* 25 (1966): 95–104.

Robinson, H. Wheeler. "The Theological Validity of Prophecy." In *Inspiration and Revelation in the Old Testament*, pp. 187–91. Oxford: Clarendon, 1953.

Wolff, Hans Walter. "How Can We Recognize False Prophets?" In *Confrontations with Prophets*, pp. 63–76. Philadelphia: Fortress, 1983.

Young, Edward J. "Prophets False and True." In *My Servants the Prophets*, pp. 125–52. Grand Rapids: Eerdmans, 1955.

3

Recognize That Divine Truth Comes in Our Kind of Word Packages

The language and vocabulary of the prophetic portions of the Bible are neither as simple and straightforward as some suppose, nor as difficult and obscure as others allege. The truth of the matter is that the biblical prophecies contain both direct prose (e.g., in the many narrative sections and some of the sermons) and figurative poetry.

The prose materials are rich in allusions to contemporary life and times. Almost always their messages are set against the backdrop of the nation's past history or its present situation. The word of God was not dropped into a cultural or historical vacuum; indeed, it was deliberately tied into the hard realities of history, geography, and the peoples of the times.

Nevertheless, side by side with all this prose writing are numerous examples of figures of speech, poetic style, symbols and symbolical actions, and visions of all sorts. These are the items which make the language of the prophets so vivid and yet so difficult to understand.

We should note here that prophecy may be simply de-

fined as the content of the special revelations which specially called men received and by which they explained
the past, elucidated the present, and disclosed the future.
These specially called men were brought into the inner
council of God by means of dreams, visions, oral com-
munications, symbolic actions, and inward suggestion. So
intimately and inextricably were the personalities of these
men interwoven with the exact statement of what God
wanted to reveal that this union could best be described
as one in which the Holy Spirit taught (not dictated in a
mechanical fashion) them in words which he wanted to
say (1 Cor. 2:13).

Given so many different authors writing over so many
years, one would expect prophecy to be little more than
a collection of aphoristic predictions and sagacious sayings. But prophecy has a definite organic nature to it. More
than focusing on particular unrelated facts, the prophets
keenly sensed their participation in an ongoing dialogue
in the progress of revelation. Such a continuity can best
be seen in the way that God's promise with all its specifications, such as the messianic seed, the land, and the
gospel for all the nations of the earth, continued to inform
all their thinking and writing.

The language and the thinking of the prophets had their
own particular perspective. It is accurate to say both that
the prophets' words were closely connected with the history of the times and that they had a unique prophetic
perspective which compressed events, sweeping massive
amounts of time into the space of a brief horizon. This
unique perspective had the effect of foreshortening the
prophet's horizon so that the near event appeared to be
joined to the distant future event with hardly any space or
time between them, much as a near and a distant mountain may from certain vantage points appear to have little
or no space between them. Both events shared so intimately in God's single program that the prophets stressed

the way they belonged to each other and were related in the great all-embracing promise-plan of God.

Of course the prophets frequently chose to express themselves in figurative and symbolic language. It would be erroneous, however, to assume that such usage implied an esoteric code of meanings that departed from the normal usage of language. As a rule, it is best to begin with the assumption that the language of the prophets is to be understood naturally; and if there is any departure from that standard, these exceptions will be warranted by earlier examples where the precise meanings of these departures from normal usage were explained.

While the prophets often clothed their thoughts in terms or formulae belonging to an earlier period of revelation, this does not mean that their thoughts failed to transcend what had been previously spoken. Nor does this tie with the past mean that they could not transcend their own historical and cultural limitations. In fact, they frequently related the past and present to the unseen future under the guidance of the Holy Spirit. In some cases the range of reference was from the creation in the past to the new heavens and the new earth in the eternity which was to come.

One of the most challenging forms of prophetic discourse is apocalyptic. This form is found, for example, in Daniel 7–12; Zechariah 1–6; Matthew 24–25; 2 Thessalonians 1; and Revelation. Its style is generally figurative. Its information is often conveyed in an announcement by angels, visions, or other supernatural means. Apocalyptic is also rich in the use of symbolic imagery. It is not unusual to meet four-headed beasts, seas of blood, bowls of wrath, and froglike spirits. Surely all of this adds to our interest and increases the vividness of the material, but it tends to frighten most interpreters away when it comes time to say what all of this means.

Apocalyptic certainly leaves the mind with a firmly imprinted image. It has the same effect on the mind as that oft-repeated experiment in which a room is darkened and then a candle lit. If we stare at the flame for a while and then close our eyes, we still see the flame, for the impression remains. The image of the flame on the mind actually outlives the visual experience. Similarly, images tend to stay with us longer than do words and the factual information they convey. Herein lie the power and the uniqueness of apocalyptic.

Because of this symbolic imagery, many lay readers avoid the apocalyptic sections of the Bible. But no matter how strange the symbolism may at first seem, it is not completely impenetrable. There are a number of keys for unlocking what may appear at first to be an enigma defying solution by the ordinary reader. We begin by noting that symbols fall into three different categories: (1) symbols that are definitely explained in the context by the writer or an interpreting angel; (2) symbols that are unexplained in the context, but are drawn from an Old Testament background; and (3) symbols that are unexplained and novel in character, but that may be drawn from the contemporary culture, including pagan sources.

Table 2 **Symbols Explained**

Symbol	Explanation	Reference
Head of gold	Nebuchadnezzar	Dan. 2:37–38
Silver arms and chest	Medo-Persia	Dan. 2:39
Rock cut out of a mountain	Kingdom of God	Dan. 2:44–45
Ten horns of fourth beast (kingdom)	Ten kings	Dan. 7:24
Two-horned ram	Medo-Persian kings	Dan. 8:20
Shaggy goat	King of Greece	Dan. 8:21
Large horn	First king of Greece	Dan. 8:21
Two olive trees	Joshua, Zerubbabel	Zech. 4:14
Woman in a bushel	Iniquity of the land	Zech. 5:6
Seven stars	Angels of the churches	Rev. 1:20
Seven lampstands	Seven churches of Asia	Rev. 1:20
Seven lamps of fire	Seven spirits of God	Rev. 4:5
Bowls of incense	Prayers of the saints	Rev. 5:8
Great dragon	Satan, devil	Rev. 12:9
Ten horns of the beast	Ten kings	Rev. 17:12
The woman	The great city	Rev. 17:18

1. *Symbols explained.* The fact that the writer explained some of his symbols and not others puzzles us. He apparently felt that some would be clearer than others, and so he offered help where the prophecy seemed obscure either to himself or to the hearers of his message when he first delivered it. Table 2 lists some of the symbols various writers explained. We ought to note the fairly consistent and uniform way in which many of these symbols are treated within each of these books. Also of interest is that some of the explained symbols are also found with the same meaning in earlier books in the Scriptures.

2. *Symbols paralleled by Old Testament imagery.* Old Testament imagery is a most important clue in interpreting prophecy. The symbols of the earlier prophets and writers seem to be used over and over again, thus forming a veritable glossary which is of immense value wherever the context suggests that the uses of the various symbols are the same.

If those scholars who suggest that Joel is among the earliest of the Old Testament writing prophets (coming in the ninth century B.C.) are correct, then his images head the list, and others borrowed copiously from him. Joel refers to "blood and fire and billows of smoke" (2:30), "the sun . . . turned to darkness and the moon to blood" (2:31), the "gather[ing of] all nations and . . . judgment against them" (3:2), the "beat[ing of] plowshares into swords and . . . pruning hooks into spears" (3:10), and "the mountains . . . drip[ping with] new wine, and the hills . . . flow[ing] with milk" (3:18).

The Book of Revelation in particular makes extensive use of the Old Testament (see table 3). This use of symbols implies a similarity to and continuity with the Old Testament message. While later revelation may feature a composite symbol for what the Old Testament divided up into several images, the essential message can still be seen. This background information is most helpful in shaping our understanding of the content and progress of prophecy.

3. *Symbols generally unexplained.* Although many

symbols are explained in the context and others are paralleled in the Old Testament, there is also a large number
of novel, vivid symbols that are left unexplained. Table 4
lists several from the Book of Revelation.

Some of these symbols can be explained by local custom
or the immediate context of the culture of that day. For
example, the white stone may well be explained as the
ballot used in a voting urn or as a pebble which was handed
out as a ticket for free entertainment. It also may have
functioned as the pebble cast by a juryman in acquitting
a prisoner. Likewise, the pillar has reference to the colon-
nades which supported the roofs and graced the porches
of the Roman temples. Therefore, each believer is being
likened to a stately pillar; only here it is in God's house
and not in some Roman temple.

Table 3 **Old Testament Symbols Used
in the Book of Revelation**

Symbol in Revelation	Old Testament Reference
The tree of life (2:7; 22:2)	Gen. 2:9; 3:24
Hidden manna (2:17)	Num. 11:7–9
Iron scepter (2:27)	Ps. 2:9
Morning star (2:28)	Dan. 12:3
Key of David (3:7)	Isa. 22:22
The living creatures (4:7–9)	Ezek. 1:5–14
The four horsemen (6:1–8)	Zech. 1:8–11
The great angel (chap. 10)	Zech. 1:11
First beast (13:1–10)	Dan. 7:2–7
Second beast (13:11–18)	Dan. 7:2–7

Table 4 **Some Unexplained Symbols in the Book of Revelation**

Symbol	Reference
White stone	Rev. 2:17
Pillar	Rev. 3:12
The twenty-four elders	Rev. 4:4, 10–11
The seven seals	Rev. 5:1; chap. 6; 8:1
Two witnesses	Rev. 11:3–12
The woman clothed with the sun	Rev. 12
The wedding of the Lamb	Rev. 19:7–9

The symbols of the prophetic sections of Scripture, and especially of apocalyptic, are not constructed out of whole cloth, but are related to realities, or at least literary references, known to the first audience that heard these messages. The largest source by far was the Old Testament, followed by the cultural symbols of the day. A lesser source consisted of the mythological figures of paganism and the apocryphal works of the period. Of course the adoption of these graphic images in no way attributed inspiration or authoritativeness to them.

Naturally, there is still an air of mystery about some of these symbols in spite of our best efforts to elucidate their meaning. This is not a totally surprising turn of events, for only as the time of fulfilment approaches will the meanings of some of these symbols become clear. There remains, of course, more than enough material for us to digest in spite of this small area of mystery and lack of precision resulting from our being removed in space and time from the original proclamation.

In addition to symbols there is still another matter that must be treated when we talk about the fact that divine truth is encapsulated in our kind of word packages. Our vocabularies are much too small to function adequately for all that we need to say. Even though most Americans have a working vocabulary of between fifteen and twenty thousand words, we would need about ninety thousand words if we were to assign a separate vocabulary entry for each referent or idea we express. This is not practical. Consequently we tend to make most of our words do triple, quadruple, or even heavier duty. The same was true of the writers of Scripture.

Thus, certain words which constantly recur in prophecy do not always have the same value. The word *earth* can stand for the whole world or for the land of Israel. The knowledge that a word may have more than one meaning is critical in interpreting a verse like Isaiah 24:1: "See, the LORD is going to lay waste the earth." Some scholars, after an examination of the context of the whole chapter, feel that the text is talking about the more restricted sense of the land of Israel. But the use of the word *world* (*tēbēl*) in verse 4 seems to point to a universal reference. Normally, a good rule of thumb is that when "earth" is used in distinction from heaven, it has the wider meaning of the whole world; when "earth" is distinguished from the Gentile world, it probably has the more narrow reference of the land of Judah or Israel.

Another good example is the word *sea*. In Daniel 7:2 the image of "the great sea" obviously stands not for the Mediterranean, but for the multitude of people out of which arose the successive world empires. Similarly, the reference to the extent of the messianic realm as being "from sea to sea" (Ps. 72:8) is not an allusion just to the boundaries of the land of Israel going from the Dead Sea to the Mediterranean Sea; rather, it points to the extremities of the oceans and the whole earth in between, an interpretation confirmed by the parallel phrase, "from the River [i.e., the Euphrates] to the ends of the earth."

Likewise the darkening of the sun with the consequent effect on its reflector, the moon, and the falling of the stars, may point to a real darkness or to times of great national or worldwide catastrophe (see Joel 2:31; 3:15; Isa. 13:10; 34:4; Ezek. 32:7; Matt. 24:29; Rev. 6:12–13).

"Fire" may be a reference to God himself—he is called a consuming fire in Deuteronomy 9:3 and Hebrews 12:29— or to his anger, which will consume the ungodly (Isa. 1:31; 66:24; Jer. 4:4; Mal. 4:1; Matt. 3:12). Yet that fire may also be purgative and not retributive, referring only to testing an individual's faith (1 Pet. 1:7). But 2 Peter 3:7 and 12 appear to predict a literal fire by which the world will finally be judged and destroyed.

These are only a few samples of the scope of prophetic thought and the forms it was cast into. Once again we must acknowledge that divine truth can come to us only through the medium of our human words. The realities to which these weak earthen vessels point burst the fragile containers in which they must necessarily be transported. Meanwhile, we must give all diligence as we study the biblical words, remembering that they point to something far richer and better than what they inadequately convey. Since there is no other way for us to receive the sacred mysteries, we shall get our best view of the divine mind if we pay close attention to what those who stood in the divine council learned as they were led and taught in words by the Holy Spirit.

For Further Study

Gasque, W. Ward. "Apocalyptic Literature." In *Zondervan Pictorial Encyclopedia of the Bible,* ed. Merrill C. Tenney, vol. 1, pp. 200–4. Grand Rapids: Zondervan, 1975.

Green, Joel B. "Prophecy as Genre," and "Symbolism: The Prophet's Tool." In *How to Read Prophecy,* pp. 49–81. Downers Grove, Ill.: Inter-Varsity, 1984.

Morris, Leon. *Apocalyptic,* pp. 9–101. Grand Rapids: Eerdmans, 1972.

Ramm, Bernard. "The Interpretation of Prophecy." In *Protestant Biblical Interpretation,* 3d ed., pp. 241–75. Grand Rapids: Baker, 1970.

Tenney, Merrill C. "The Symbolism of Revelation." In *Interpreting Revelation,* pp. 186–93. Grand Rapids: Eerdmans, 1957.

4

Go Back to the Past
in Order to Get to the Future

It sounds strange, but it is true: prophecy is best understood by going back into the past in order to perceive what God is going to do in the future. So significant is this advice for the reader and interpreter of prophecy that we have entitled this book *Back Toward the Future.*

Of all the various forms of prophetic thought, few are so common and so helpful in getting a handle on the meaning as the writer's borrowing past events, persons, or expressions to depict the future. The reason for choosing to use what appears at first so strange is simple: no one has ever been in the future, so how can the writer adequately talk about or the reader understand what neither has ever experienced? But if the future bears certain analogies to the historic past and if God's method of operation has a consistency and pattern to it, borrowing the past in order to help us conceptualize the future is a most logical way of proceeding.

The comparisons between the historic past and the future may be formal and direct, or allusive and indirect. Of course the future is not exactly comparable to the past, for

51

that would flatten out Scripture and yield no progress in the plan and revelation of God. There is, however, just enough similarity between the past and the future that one who has never been there can begin to imagine what is being talked about.

Let us take some of the events mentioned in the first five books of the Bible, the Pentateuch, and note how these events were used in the prophets for predictive purposes. The following list was compiled by Robert B. Girdlestone in his grand volume entitled *The Grammar of Prophecy.* In chapter 9, "The Future Expressed in Terms of the Past," Girdlestone observes that the prophets used seven notable past events to set forth their predictions about the future: (1) creation, (2) life in paradise, (3) the flood, (4) the destruction of Sodom and Gomorrah, (5) the Egyptian bondage, (6) the exodus, and (7) the wilderness wanderings. Each of these events served as a paradigm of what God was going to do in the future.

1. *Creation.* One of the most fundamental truths in Scripture is that God made the heavens and the earth merely by speaking them into existence by the word of his mouth (notice the statement repeated ten times over in Gen. 1, "And God said," along with such theological formulations as Ps. 33:6, 9; Heb. 11:3).

But there will also be new heavens and a new earth. What will these be like and how will they come into being? The prophet Isaiah informs us in Isaiah 65:17 and 66:22. God will create them. Second Peter 3:13 links this new work of God with his old word of promise, and in Revelation 21:1 the whole process is declared as good as accomplished. The point is, of course, that the new is accomplished much as the old was: by the word of the Lord. Both the old and the new creations are the result of the direct work and word of God. To know the present creation is to know in some sense what the new creation will be like, for they are both from the hands of the same loving Lord.

2. *Paradise.* God placed Adam and Eve in the Garden of Eden (Gen. 2:8). There, with the tree of life in the midst and with the rivers flowing out to the surrounding regions, God set a standard for the paradisiacal conditions which he intended for the men and women he created.

The aspiration for the full realization of these conditions was not totally discarded when the original couple fell into sin. Instead, the description of the joys experienced here set the norm for what our Lord declared to be his goal for the future conditions of the redeemed when he restores all things at his coming again. In Isaiah 51:3 we have a direct comparison between the comforts of Eden and what God intends for the new Jerusalem: "The LORD will surely comfort Zion and will look with compassion on all her ruins; he will make her deserts like Eden, her wastelands like the garden of the LORD" (see also Zech. 1:17).

Not only is the promise of paradise held out for the towns and regions of Israel, it is held out in the New Testament to all believers. The apostle John writes to the church at Ephesus, "To him who overcomes, I will give the right to eat from the tree of life, which is in the paradise of God" (Rev. 2:7). The full accomplishment of that promise appears to be attained in the new heaven and the new earth and new Jerusalem described in Revelation 22:1–2, where the river of the water of life flows from the throne of God, and on each side of the river there stands a tree of life. Paradise is more than just a memory; it is the standard by which our Lord will correct what we sinners have spoiled and ruined by our sin. There will be new life, living waters flowing from the stream of God, and the tree of life, which will not only symbolize the prospect of life, but now will participate in its reality!

3. *The flood.* The answer to the question, "What will God's coming judgment against all sinners who finally and totally reject him be like?" can be found close at hand in the experience of Noah and his generation. After Noah had preached and begged his generation to turn from their

wicked ways (some say for over one hundred years), God
finally sent a flood that took every life on planet earth
except for the eight people who believed and went on board
the ark. No doubt Noah took a lot of abuse and was the
brunt of numerous cruel jokes for his dedication to build-
ing an enormous tublike contraption out in the middle of
nowhere, far away from any good-sized body of water.

But the lesson learned there in Genesis 6–8 would serve
as a warning to all future generations. The flood was also
the occasion of God's making a new promise to the human
race. Isaiah made a plain comparison when as the spokes-
man of God he wrote: "To me this is like the days of Noah,
when I swore that the waters of Noah would never again
cover the earth. So now I have sworn not to be angry with
you, never to rebuke you again. . . . My covenant [will not]
be removed" (54:9–10). "Never again," the Lord had promised in Genesis 8:21, "will I destroy all living creatures as
I have done."

However, this is not to say that the wicked conditions
that had brought on the flood would never be seen again.
Indeed, our Lord warned during his earthly ministry: "As
it was in the days of Noah, so it will be at the coming of
the Son of Man. For in the days before the flood, people
were eating and drinking, marrying and giving in marriage,
up to the day Noah entered the ark; and they knew nothing about what would happen until the flood came and
took them all away. That is how it will be at the coming
of the Son of Man" (Matt. 24:37–39). The old skepticism
will return again; the scoffers will sneer, "Where is this
'coming' he promised?" But what they willingly choose to
forget, warns Peter in 2 Peter 3:3–7, is that the world was
destroyed in a flood by the word of God. The next time it
will be destroyed by fire.

4. *The destruction of Sodom and Gomorrah.* God rained
down fire and brimstone on the five cities of the plain
because they willfully chose to ignore God and his standard of righteousness. This act became a sample and a

type of God's dealings with all who are finally and totally unrepentant after constantly refusing the grace, mercy, and goodness of God which could and should have led them to repentance (see Gen. 18–19; Deut. 29:23).

Isaiah, once again, illustrates how this ancient word was picked up and used to describe God's new work. In Isaiah 1:9 he chided, "Unless the LORD Almighty had left us some survivors, we would have become like Sodom, we would have been like Gomorrah." Then in a bold change of address, he exhorted the leaders and the citizens of Judah to pay attention, for they were in real danger of becoming exactly what God had rebuked in the five cities of the plain. So real was their danger, Isaiah addressed them as if they were those cities. He declared, "Hear the word of the LORD, you rulers of Sodom; listen to the law of our God, you people of Gomorrah!" (v. 10).

Likewise in the Book of Revelation, John shows how the same spirit will infect the populace of Jerusalem after they hear the urgent summons for them to abandon their sins and to repent. Their response will be to rise up and murder the two witnesses, leaving the bodies to rot in the streets while they celebrate by sending gifts to one another. John comments, the bodies of these two witnesses "lie in the street of the great city, which is figuratively called Sodom and Egypt, where also their Lord was crucified" (Rev. 11:8).

There are many other places where Sodom and Gomorrah appear in the prophets. Jeremiah complains that the false prophets of his day "are all like Sodom to [the Lord]; the people of Jerusalem are like Gomorrah" (Jer. 23:14). Israel is likened to Sodom once again in Ezekiel 16:49–50. But, surprisingly, God will restore the fortunes of this new Sodom if they only repent (16:53).

Both Sodom and Gomorrah still face an even worse judgment on the final day. But "it will be more bearable for Sodom and Gomorrah on the day of judgment" than for those cities that witnessed firsthand the words and works of the Son of God (Matt. 10:15; 11:24).

"The LORD rained down burning sulfur on Sodom and Gomorrah—from the LORD out of the heavens" (Gen. 19:24). This language became a way of describing the physical fate that awaits the ungodly. Did not David write, "On the wicked he will rain fiery coals and burning sulfur" (Ps. 11:6)? Similarly, when Gog attacks the land of Israel in the future, God "will pour down torrents of rain, hailstones and burning sulfur on him and on his troops and on the many nations with him" (Ezek. 38:22).

It was this same vocabulary that supplied the descriptions of "the fiery lake of burning sulfur" (Rev. 19:20) and the judgment on everyone who worships the beast: "He will be tormented with burning sulfur. . . . And the smoke of their torment rises for ever and ever" (Rev. 14:10–11). That is precisely the point made in Jude 7—"In a similar way, Sodom and Gomorrah and the surrounding towns gave themselves up to sexual immorality and perversion. They serve as an example of those who suffer the punishment of eternal fire." The realities of the judgments of Sodom and Gomorrah should not be lightly passed over, for the same Lord will inspect the lives of all in that coming day, and there will follow as sure a judgment.

5. *The Egyptian bondage.* The plagues on Egypt would come on Israel as well if they disobeyed, warned Moses in Deuteronomy 28:27, 60. Moreover, Israel would once again be subject to bondage: "The LORD will send you back in ships to Egypt on a journey I said you should never make again. There you will offer yourselves for sale to your enemies as male and female slaves, but no one will buy you" (Deut. 28:68).

An identical warning was voiced by the prophet Hosea—"They will return to Egypt" (Hos. 8:13); "Ephraim will return to Egypt and eat unclean food in Assyria" (Hos. 9:3). In other words, the predicted Assyrian captivity was but Egypt revisited; it was bondage all over again, only in a different geographical location. "Egypt will gather them, and Memphis will bury them" (Hos. 9:6), warned the prophet. Assyria would become a second Egypt: "Will they not return to Egypt and will not Assyria rule over them because they refuse to repent?" (Hos. 11:5). As a consequence of their sins, Israel was liable to the same punishment that had brought the destruction of Sodom and Gomorrah and the plagues on Egypt. Amos wrote, " 'I sent plagues among you as I did to Egypt. . . . I overthrew some of you as I overthrew Sodom and Gomorrah. . . . Yet you have not returned to me,' declares the LORD" (Amos 4:10–11). Likewise, the reappearance of the plagues in the Book of Revelation is not surprising, given what we have seen thus far as to how God works.

6. *The exodus.* Just as God miraculously took Israel across the Red Sea, so there will be another exodus in a future day. In that day "the LORD will dry up the gulf of the Egyptian sea . . . so that men can cross over in sandals" (Isa. 11:15). That exodus, however, will not be limited to a departure from Egypt; it will start "from the four quarters of the earth" (Isa. 11:12). The song of praise that will follow this new exodus in that future day (Isa. 12:2) is based on Moses' song in Exodus 15:2, and so Israel "will sing as in the days of her youth, as in the day she came up out of Egypt" (Hos. 2:15).

Long after Judah had returned from the seventy years of exile in Babylon, the prophet Zechariah in 518 B.C. was still anticipating another return of the nation. The Lord promised, "I will bring them back from Egypt and gather them from Assyria. . . . They will pass through the sea of trouble; . . . and all the depths of the Nile will dry up. Assyria's pride will be brought down and Egypt's scepter will pass away" (Zech. 10:10–11). Many of us believe that that restoration will yet take place for the nation of Israel. Yet the language used to describe it recalls God's first great restoration from Egypt.

7. *The wilderness wanderings.* Especially significant

during the forty years of trekking through the desert was
the presence of the Lord symbolized in the pillar of cloud
by day, which became a pillar of fire by night. The form
of the divine overshadowing at that time became the basic
image describing the real presence of the Lord on Mount
Zion in that future day. Isaiah 4:5–6 glows with pride as
it announces, "[In that day] the LORD will create over all
of Mount Zion and over those who assemble there a cloud
of smoke by day and a glow of flaming fire by night; over
all the glory will be a canopy. It will be a shelter and shade
from the heat of the day, and a refuge and hiding place
from the storm and rain."

In addition to the pillar of cloud and fire, streams of
water will break out in the desert; God will make the
desert blossom once again in connection with the events
of his return (Isa. 35:6–7; 43:19). The same Lord will once
again make a new way in the desert as he leads his people
back home.

It is clear, then, that the prophets and the New Testament depended on many of the experiences in the Pentateuch for the basic vocabulary and images to describe what
God was going to do in the future. To the degree that we
appreciate God's work and words in the past, we are given
insight into the future.

The prophets use not only historic events to portray the
future, but also historic persons as well. For example, Elijah is used by Malachi: "See, I will send you the prophet
Elijah before that great and dreadful day of the LORD comes"
(Mal. 4:5).

It would appear that Elijah may be one of the two witnesses who will yet minister during those awful days described in Revelation 11. But in the meantime, Elijah has
already come, or at least his spirit and power have come
(Luke 1:17), in the person of John the Baptist (Matt. 11:14).
Yet the Baptist is not the complete fulfilment of this prediction, for our Lord's exposition of Elijah's coming (Matt.

17:11–13) involves both a present and a future aspect. (For a discussion of the two ages of predictive teaching—the present age ["now"] and the age to come ["not yet"]—see chapter 10.)

There were other individuals who pointed to prominent persons and events that would follow in their train. The office and authority of all who were in the line of David, of course, pointed to the Messiah and his reign which was to come. What had gone before prefigured what was to come.

Perhaps the best way to summarize this strange phenomenon of going forward by going backward is to examine a relevant passage from the prophets. For this purpose we have chosen Haggai 2:20–23. In order to describe God's marvelous future deliverance "on that day," Haggai reaches back to God's great acts in the past. As he "overthrew" Sodom and Gomorrah once (Gen. 18–19), so in that future day he will "overturn royal thrones and shatter the power of the foreign kingdoms" (Hag. 2:22). The past helps us to conceptualize the future. But there is more. Just as the horse and the rider went down into the Red Sea (Exod. 15:1, 5), so God "will overthrow chariots and their drivers; horses and their riders will fall" (Hag. 2:22). "Each by the sword of his brother" will be vanquished in that day, just as Gideon stood still and watched the Midianites polish off one another (Judg. 7:22; cf. Ezek. 38:21; Zech. 14:13). Once again it is God who will act; Judah will have no need to fight to defend herself as God wins a great victory singlehandedly.

Haggai ends his declaration of this future victory by announcing that God will choose another member of the line of David to bear the signet ring. The "signet ring" had been taken from King Jehoiachin (Jer. 22:24–27), David's son through Solomon's line, and given instead to another one of David's descendants through his son Nathan. But the messianic line was preserved; and the seal, authority, and legitimacy of the government that was to come were maintained and reserved for Jesus.

Our Lord has been able to communicate with us about the future even though we have never seen any of its realities. Since he is Lord of history, the past is a wonderful ticket into the future. The language of prophecy is not as strange and as enigmatic as we at first think. Once we come to know his-story, we come to know his future.

For Further Study

Fairbairn, Patrick. "Combination of Type with Prophecy." In *The Typology of Scripture*, pp. 106–39. Grand Rapids: Baker, 1975.

Foulkes, Francis. *The Acts of God: A Study of the Basis of Typology in the Old Testament*, pp. 7–40. London: Tyndale, 1958.

Girdlestone, Robert B. "The Future Expressed in Terms of the Past." In *The Grammar of Prophecy: A Systematic Guide to Biblical Prophecy*, pp. 66–75. Grand Rapids: Kregel, 1955.

Gowan, Donald E. *Eschatology in the Old Testament*, pp. 1–129. Philadelphia: Fortress, 1986.

5

Remember: *Sometimes* *"It All Depends"*

How could anyone qualify any of God's words by saying, "It all depends"? Wouldn't such a qualification immediately steal from the authority and dignity that rightfully belong to our Lord? But that is the dilemma that the category of conditional prophecies appears to raise. It looks as if God first declared what would happen in the future only to be second-guessed and outmaneuvered by mere mortals who had other plans in mind.

Scripture, it is true, does distinguish a special category which we may label as conditional prophecies. The fulfillment of these predictions is dependent and contingent on certain actions and responses of men and women. Our difficulty comes from an inadequate view of God and from a failure to understand that the conditions contained in these prophecies are an integral part of God's intent.

To begin with, God is not some changeless impersonal force that is incapable of responding in a vital way to changes in others. Impersonal changelessness has no relation to the God and Father of our Lord Jesus Christ. Our God can and does respond to human persons in a vital way. His own words to Pharaoh document the possibility of change: "For by now I could have stretched out my hand and struck you and your people with a plague that would have wiped you off the earth. But I have raised you up for this very purpose, that I might show you my power and that my name might be proclaimed in all the earth" (Exod. 9:15–16). It is not that God's standards, his nature, or his character changes, but that as a living person he can and does change when people change, either accepting or rejecting what he has set forth as the norm of righteousness.

While some of the prophecies of Scripture are absolute and capable of no change because they depend solely upon God for their fulfilment, others have alternative prospects attached to them. In Leviticus 26 and Deuteronomy 28, for example, God pledges blessings if Israel obeys, but punishment if they disobey.

Another example is the prospect which Jeremiah laid before King Zedekiah, "If you surrender to the officers of the king of Babylon, your life will be spared and this city will not be burned down; you and your family will live. But if you will not surrender to the officers of the king of Babylon, this city will be handed over to the Babylonians and they will burn it down; you yourself will not escape from their hands" (Jer. 38:17–18). Unfortunately Zedekiah chose the second alternative and found the prophecy to be true. This, then, is a case where the conditions were plainly spelled out and set forth as two different ways in which the person affected could go. Even though the text might not always spell out the alternatives or the conditional nature of the prediction, many prophecies fit into this category in that they are addressed to mortals who must make a choice.

Jeremiah 42:10–16 is another passage where two alternatives are set before the people—"If you stay in this land [of Judah], I will build you up and not tear you down. . . . However, if you say, 'We will not stay in this land,' and so disobey the LORD your God, and if you say, 'No, we will go and live in Egypt, where we will not see war or hear the trumpet or be hungry for bread,' . . . then the sword you fear will overtake you there, and the famine you dread will follow you into Egypt, and there you will die." The people chose the latter and died as a result.

Not always was the conditional nature of a prediction plainly stated in Scripture. Isaiah's message to King Hezekiah, for instance, was quite straightforward, "This is what the LORD says: Put your house in order, because you are going to die; you will not recover" (2 Kings 20:1). That seems clear enough! On the face of it there do not seem to be any ands, ifs, or buts. Hezekiah would not recover, period!

Hezekiah, however, turned his face to the wall, wept bitterly, and prayed. Before the prophet Isaiah had left the palace courtyard, the Lord instructed him to return and to give a new word from the Lord: "This is what the LORD, the God of your father David, says: I have heard your prayer and seen your tears; I will heal you. . . . I will add fifteen years to your life" (2 Kings 20:5–6).

Prophecies were intended to motivate mortals into conformity with divine holiness. Since Isaiah's solemn word had moved Hezekiah's heart toward God in prayer, it was possible for God, while not changing *in his character*, to change *in his actions* towards Hezekiah. It is this attribute which allows God, given an appropriate change in the recipient(s) of a prophetic utterance, to depart from fulfilling what he has said he will do and to move to an alternate course of action.

The clearest statement of this principle can be found in Jeremiah 18:7–10:

> If at any time I announce that a nation or kingdom is to be uprooted, torn down and destroyed, and if that nation I warned repents of its evil, then I will relent and not inflict on it the disaster I had planned. And if at another time I announce that a nation or kingdom is to be built up and planted, and if it does evil in my sight and does not obey

me, then I will reconsider the good I had intended to do
for it.

Notice that the statement is put into a universal form: it
does not apply just to Judah or to Israel; it is true of any
nation or kingdom. Notice also that the words of destruction or of blessing are not automatically carried out on the
nation to whom these words have been addressed; everything depends on what that nation does with respect to
the laws of God.

This principle explains why Jonah was so reluctant to
go and announce God's imminent judgment on the nation
of Assyria and its capital of Nineveh. If judgment were
only forty days away, reasoned Jonah, the populace might
suddenly get the idea that they should repent. Then the
threatened judgment would be withdrawn, and the hated
Assyrians would have escaped Israel's clutches once again.
Jonah had to be operating on the principle announced later
on in Jeremiah 18:7–10, for nothing else explains his stub-
bornness and intransigence.

Jeremiah himself had frequent occasion to witness the
implementation of this conditional principle. When the
priests and prophets wanted to have him killed, he warned:
"The LORD sent me to prophesy against this house and
this city all the things you have heard. Now reform your
ways and your actions and obey the LORD your God. Then
the LORD will relent and not bring the disaster he has
pronounced against you" (Jer. 26:12–13). Once again it is
clear: if the people would repent (i.e., turn from their sin),
then God would repent (i.e., relent). The grounds of his
reversal of action would be his eternal attributes and the
promises that he had made in his word to the patriarchs
and to all who believe him. Prominent among those qual-
ities of the eternal God is his mercy. Accordingly, Jeremiah
preached: " 'Return [i.e.,repent], faithless Israel, . . . for I
am merciful,' declares the LORD" (Jer. 3:12). Even more
graphically Hosea pleads, "How can I give you up, Ephraim?

How can I hand you over, Israel? . . . My heart is changed within me; all my compassion is aroused" (Hos. 11:8).

Revelation repeatedly affirms that God is slow to anger and most merciful; he will turn aside from his anger whenever men and women make it possible for him to do so by repenting of their sins before him. It is this aspect of his gracious character that accounts for the category of conditional prophecies.

When can the reader and interpreter assume that they are dealing with a conditional prophecy? Some have suggested two helpful guidelines. A prophecy is conditional (1) if it refers to an event which is fairly proximate in time and space, and (2) if it is capable of being answered by some act of obedience or repentance on the part of the prophet's contemporaries.

These two guidelines for conditional prophecies fit the case of Jonah perfectly. Jonah's famous oracle, "Forty more days and Nineveh will be overturned" (Jon. 3:4), involves both an imminent event and the possibility of repentance on the part of those against whom the word was delivered. The reason this word was delivered was the wickedness of the city of Nineveh (Jon. 1:2). When the Ninevites reacted by "call[ing] urgently on God [and] giv[ing] up their evil ways and their violence" (Jon. 3:8), God was able to change and not bring on them the judgment he had threatened (Jon. 3:10). This case is an outstanding model of exactly what happens when the alternatives are only implicitly affixed to the prediction.

What is exhibited here concerning the life of a nation is true on an individual level as well. When Elijah threatened King Ahab of Israel with what looked to be certain punishment ("In the place where dogs licked up Naboth's blood, dogs will lick up your blood—yes, yours!" 1 Kings 21:19), Ahab tore his clothes in grief, fasted, put on sackcloth, and went around meekly before the Lord (1 Kings 21:27). Such a change in the indicted man brought a corresponding change in God, who informed Elijah, "Because he has humbled himself, I will not bring this disaster in his day" (v. 29). And so it was. Without Elijah's saying that his prophecy was conditional, Ahab acted on the assumption that it fell in that category, and it turned out that he was correct. Ezekiel 33:13–16 applies to individuals the fixed principle which Jeremiah 18:7–10 had applied to nations. The actual fulfilment of prophecy depends on the moral and spiritual condition of those to whom the word was spoken.

Thus hundreds of prophecies that appear to be absolute are actually conditional. Their words were never fulfilled in the manner in which they were first stated since the words came as a warning and produced some results, albeit ever so slight and temporary in many cases.

Regrettably, the very presence of conditional prophecies in the Bible has encouraged some interpreters to classify as conditional many predictions which are actually absolute and without any kind of condition whatsoever. This danger is particularly acute in the case of prophecies concerning the land of Israel, prophecies which some scholars regard as obsolete as a result of Israel's failure to obey. However, such prophecies are not conditional, for they do not meet the two guidelines mentioned earlier: imminency and contingency on a response from the addressees. Furthermore, the prophecies about the land are closely identified with the promise of the Seed (i.e., the Messiah) and the promise of the gospel ("in thy seed shall all the nations of the earth be blessed," Gen. 22:18 KJV; cf. Gal. 3:8); and God took completely on himself the obligation for their fulfilment. Since the offer of the Messiah and the gospel is not subject to withdrawal or revocation, neither can the offer of the land to Israel be withdrawn. All three features are said to be "eternal."

It is true, of course, that *participation* in the promise was by an act of faith, but this must not be confused with the *provision* of the promise of the Messiah, the gospel, or the land. The promises in this case are unconditional;

the participation is conditional. In fact, so certain were these promises that God confirmed his word with an oath (Gen. 22:16; Ps. 105:9; Heb. 6:17–18).

In addition to God's changing his course of action, another possible effect of the response of obedience or repentance is the delayed fulfilment of a prophecy. Thus the expected fate of Jerusalem's destruction was held back because of King Josiah's humble and sincere obedience to all that he heard when the book of the law was found. Commented Huldah the prophetess, under divine inspiration, "Because your heart was responsive and you humbled yourself before the LORD when you heard what I have spoken against this place and its people, . . . therefore I will gather you to your fathers, and you will be buried in peace. Your eyes will not see all the disaster I am going to bring on this place" (2 Kings 22:19–20).

King Josiah died in 609 B.C., which was before Daniel and his three friends were taken to Babylon in the first captivity (606), Ezekiel was exiled (598), and Jerusalem fell (587). What had been announced as certain was certain because very few of the populace repented. But because Josiah did respond, the prophecy of 2 Kings 22:16–17 was delayed and put on an altered schedule, even though it still came about as foretold.

Another instance of a prophecy whose fulfilment was delayed can be found in Micah 3:12. Micah's word in the eighth century had an effect on King Hezekiah and many of his day. So remarkable was the response that Jeremiah made a favorable allusion to it a century later in Jeremiah 26:18–19, "Did not Hezekiah fear the LORD and seek his favor [when Micah said, 'Zion will be plowed like a field, Jerusalem will become a heap of rubble, the temple hill a mound overgrown with thickets']? And did not the LORD relent, so that he did not bring the disaster he pronounced against them?" Thus the king's repentance obviated for the time being the fulfilment of what was a conditional prophecy from Micah. Since the repentance was not widespread, the effect was only to delay the fulfilment, for the disaster predicted eventually came in 587, when Jerusalem fell.

It must be stressed again that not all prophetic utterances are conditional. There are some things which "the LORD has sworn and [he] will not change his mind" (Ps. 110:4). In almost every case, these are the promises that have to do with God's providing our salvation. God chose a man, a family, a nation, and a people to inherit, embody, and conserve the long line of promises concerning the provision of our salvation. No sin, no failure on the part of any individual or group of persons, could ever derail or prevent God's great purpose in Christ. These gifts and this calling will always be without any repentance, change, or deviation (Rom. 11:29).

Such irreversible promises depend on God's mercy and provision and not on any individual's work. The circumstances of all the other predictions might be modified, and the time delayed or shortened, but the purpose of God and the character of God have remained fixed, sure, and consistent with all that God is in his own person.

For Further Study

Girdlestone, Robert B. "Prophecies Conditional and Unconditional." In *The Grammar of Prophecy: A Systematic Guide to Biblical Prophecy,* pp. 25–30. Grand Rapids: Kregel, 1955.

Lang, G. H. "God's Covenants Are Conditional." *Evangelical Quarterly* 32 (1958): 86–97. (Lang takes the opposite position from the one I have advocated here.)

Oxtoby, Gurdon C. "Prophecy and Prediction." In *Prediction and Fulfillment in the Bible,* pp. 62–93. Philadelphia: Westminster, 1966. (The discussions are helpful, but must be used with care.)

Payne, J. Barton. "The Necessity of Fulfillment." In *Encyclopedia of Biblical Prophecy: The Complete Guide to Scriptural Predictions and Their Fulfillment,* pp. 59–71. New York: Harper and Row, 1973; Grand Rapids: Baker, 1980.

6

Profit from the Preparation and the Skills of the Prophets

It is time we said something about those to whom the prophecies came. Who were these individuals? What explanation do they offer for the wonderful gift they exercised? What special skills did they bring, if any, to the office? How did they obtain this office, and who installed them? What was their position in the community of believers, and what was their reputation among the nations abroad? Was the gift of prophecy terminated long ago so that we may only look back on it with a nostalgic longing for the good old days when God used to make himself known in more dramatic ways?

One thing is for sure. These men and women (yes, women too!) made no pretense to any remarkable skills of their own or to any distinguished learning abilities. While they functioned as God's mouthpieces, there is never a claim that they were taught a prophetic skill, or even that they formed some guild or special caste like the priests.

There were men of learning among the ranks of the prophets, such as Moses, Daniel, and Paul. But others came from the ordinary spheres of life. They all affirmed that they had not campaigned for the position; that was the clear affirmation, for example, of Amos.

Instead, it all began with a strong sense of the call of
God. Most of the prophets had been faithfully employed
in some other work when the call of God came and changed
everything in their lives. Samuel, however, was only a lad
when God called him in such clear tones that he was
aroused from his sleep three times. Elisha was busy plow-
ing with the twelfth team of oxen in his father's fields
when he received his call to service. Jeremiah and Daniel
were both quite young when they too heard the call to
service. Ezekiel, on the other hand, had already reached
his thirtieth birthday; and Paul was deeply involved in
eliminating as many Christians as he could when he was
stopped on his way to Damascus, intending to add more
Christians to the growing numbers of martyrs. Amos was
a most successful sheepherder and farmer when he was
yanked out of those professions to follow a new career.

In no case can it be shown that the office of prophet
was connected with personal ambition or motives of profit,
influence, or pride. The prophets uniformly pointed to the
clear call of God and the heavy influence of his hand on
their lives. They had to respond, even though some at first
felt most reluctant to undertake so holy a calling.

Amos supplies some of the best insights into what a
call to be a prophet was like. It is almost as if he had not
planned on reporting how he was called, for he places it
right in the middle of a series of five visions. After the
third vision, in which the plumb line of God's righteousness reveals that Israel is clearly out of plumb morally,
Amos introduces a historical narrative (7:10–17) to show
how badly Israel and her spiritual leadership had deviated
from God's standard. The priest of Bethel, one of the two
false centers of worship for the northern kingdom, har-
assed Amos and told him to go back down south to earn
his living instead of trying to prophesy in the north. Amos
responded in the strongest terms he could muster: "I was
neither a prophet nor a prophet's son, but I was a shepherd,
and I also took care of sycamore-fig trees. But the LORD

took me from tending the flock and said to me, 'Go, prophesy to my people Israel' " (vv. 14–15).

A good number of modern scholars assert what the grammar will not permit: they claim that Amos was disassociating himself from the prophets, saying, "I am not a prophet nor a son of the prophets." However, Amos's point is that he was gainfully employed in other pursuits previously, and that his present role as a prophet is directly and solely attributable to the call of God on his life.

More traditional was the call of Isaiah. After sketching the needs of the times for a prophetic ministry (Isa. 1–5), he records his call in Isaiah 6. That call featured four key elements: (1) a theophany, that is, an appearance of God; (2) a purification of the initiate's lips; (3) a commission as to what he was to do; and (4) the content of the message he was to proclaim. So significant was this call that Isaiah was given a glimpse of the courts of heaven and the Lord Jesus Christ himself seated on a throne (cf. John 12:41). Isaiah's response to his summons to service was an immediate yes. He would be God's prophet.

Jeremiah was as reluctant and as unbending at first as was Moses when God called him. Jeremiah pleaded (1:6) that he was too young for such a high calling. In fact, though Jeremiah eventually gave in, he felt overwhelmed, severely constrained, and overpowered by the Lord when he was called; at least those were his feelings in retrospect (Jer. 20:7). Furthermore, every time he experienced bitter mockery because of his crying out the need for repentance, he determined he would abandon the whole endeavor. His countrymen ridiculed him, saying in effect, "This old preacher is a complete bore; he just has two points all the time: 'Violence and destruction' " (Jer. 20:8). But whenever Jeremiah decided that he had had enough, God revitalized the prophet so that he exclaimed, "[God's] word is in my heart like a fire. . . . I am weary of holding it in; indeed, I cannot" (Jer. 20:9). He had no choice but to proclaim the word he was given to preach.

Ezekiel was called, as was Isaiah, by a vision of the majesty, greatness, and glory of the Lord (Ezek. 1–3). His call, likewise, featured four elements: (1) a theophany; (2) a preparation for ministry which included the eating of a scroll on which was written the message he was to share (a message which tasted sweet at first, but then turned bitter in his stomach); (3) a time for his response, which included fear and trembling; and (4) a time of strengthening by the Lord. The point of the vision was that seated on the throne above the platform mounted on wheels was the living God, who promised that he would be present wherever he sent his prophet. The mighty word of prophecy was to be backed by the powerful presence of the glory of God wherever Ezekiel ministered that word.

By now it has become clear that most of these men felt extremely inadequate to carry out such a task. "Woe to me!" marveled Isaiah. "I am ruined! For I am a man of unclean lips, and I live among a people of unclean lips, and my eyes have seen the King, the LORD Almighty" (Isa. 6:5). Likewise, Jeremiah protested, "Ah, Sovereign LORD, . . . I do not know how to speak; I am only a child" (Jer. 1:6). But over and above all of these feelings there was the strong compulsion of the hand of God (Ezek. 1:3; 3:14; 8:1; Jer. 15:20).

More light can be shed on the nature of the prophetic gifts by examining some of the key Hebrew terms for "prophet." Though most of these titles were adopted by both the false and the true prophets alike, they still give us an insight into some of the tasks and ministries that the true prophets performed.

One of the earliest terms was *rō'eh* ("seer"). With regard to specific individuals we know of its usage only in connection with Samuel (1 Sam. 9:9) and Hanani (2 Chron. 16:7). The only place it occurs in the prophetic books is Isaiah 30:10. The term seems to stress God's gift of seeing what is lost (as in the case of Samuel with the donkeys of Saul's father) or what is to come in the future.

Closely aligned to this term is the second designation for a prophet, *ḥōzeh* ("visionary"). Here the focus is not on the natural eye that was given a view of the distant future or of what was lost, but on the mental or inward eye. The term appears as early as Exodus 24:11, where we are told that the seventy elders "saw" God. Balaam, the prophet from upper Mesopotamia, claimed to "see" a vision from the Almighty (Num. 24:4); but the first technical use of *ḥōzeh* is found in 2 Samuel 24:11 in connection with Gad, David's visionary. Interestingly enough, 2 Chronicles 16:7 describes the prophet Hanani as a *rō'eh*, but 2 Chronicles 19:2 refers to Hanani's son as a *ḥōzeh*. The priest of Bethel also used the term *ḥōzeh* to describe Amos in their bitter encounter in Amos 7:12.

The most significant term by far is the word *nābî'*. Most students of ancient Near Eastern languages agree that this Hebrew word probably reflects an Akkadian (the language of early Mesopotamia) word meaning "to call or to announce." The debate nowadays centers around whether the root is passive ("one who is called [by God]") or active ("an announcer"). Most of us favor the passive and therefore stress that a prophet is one who has heard the call of God for a very specific task.

If this appears to be a bit obscure, reflect for a minute on the two grand texts of Exodus 4:15–16 and 7:1 where the Lord sets up a model which ought to clarify any remaining mysteries as to how a prophet is to function. Because of Moses' protestations about his slowness of wit and tongue, God announced, "See, I have made you like God to Pharaoh, and your brother Aaron will be your prophet" (Exod. 7:1). Moses was to "speak to [Aaron] and put words in his mouth"; God promised: "I will help both of you speak and will teach you what to do" (Exod. 4:15). The important point for our purposes is that the proposed working relationship between Moses and Aaron reflects that between God and his prophets.

Earlier scholarship linked *nābî'* with a differently spelled

Arabic word meaning "to bubble forth, writhe," thus suggesting that the distinguishing mark of the prophets was an ecstatic experience and that the revelations came to them when they were in a state akin to a fit of artistic madness. However, that suggestion cannot stand up to modern linguistic tests.

The noun *nābî'* appears over three hundred times and the related verb over one hundred times. It expresses both the function and the essence of a prophet. Simply stated: a prophet delivers a message that is not his own.

We conclude, then, that a *nābî'* is one who is sent by God to announce his word. A *rō'eh* is one who is given insight into the past, present, and future. A *ḥōzeh* is given his message in a vision. Only 1 Chronicles 29:29 uses all three terms in one verse: "As for the events of King David's reign, . . . they are written in the records of Samuel the seer (*rō'eh*), the records of Nathan the prophet (*nābî'*) and the records of Gad the seer (*ḥōzeh*)."

This is not to suggest that there are no other terms for prophet; indeed there are. For example, many are called "man of God," beginning with Moses in Deuteronomy 33:1. Even more popular was the term "servant of the Lord," which also was used of Moses in Joshua 1:1. Only once was any prophet called "the Lord's messenger [angel]" (Hag. 1:13). And there were "shepherd" (Ezek. 34), "watchman" (Ezek. 33), and many other titles. But in one way or another they all stressed the prophets' relationship to God and to the mission he had given to them.

Since the main sphere of the prophets' ministry was to deliver God's word, it is appropriate for us to investigate how that word reached these called individuals. It could come (1) during the prophet's ordinary activity—as Isaiah crossed the king's courtyard, he was told to retrace his steps and deliver a message that countered the one he had just delivered; (2) in a vision—consider the case of Joseph or God's words to Aaron and Miriam in Numbers 12:6, "When a prophet of the Lord is among you, I reveal myself to him in visions, I speak to him in dreams"; or (3) in a direct encounter—God said, "With [my servant Moses] I speak face to face, clearly and not in riddles" (Num. 12:7). When Moses was on Mount Sinai for forty days, God spoke to him directly and intimately.

Dreams come to almost everyone and on occasion may serve to give warning or to suggest some course of action. Visions, on the other hand, appear to be granted solely to special persons. In a vision, heaven and the spiritual realm are presented to the mind's eye. These visions may involve well-known objects, such as an altar or an olive tree, or they may involve the supernatural, such as cherubim and manifestations of the Divine Being in all his radiant splendor. The trance (for indeed there is some sort of crossing from the physical realm to the spiritual) may be only for a short time, as it was for Micaiah (1 Kings 22:19), or for an extended period of time with the prophet bordering on unconsciousness, as in the case of Ezekiel (40–48) and the apostle John (Rev. 1–22).

Various expressions, advises Robert B. Girdlestone, identify the state of prophetic rapture.[1] Often the prophet declares, "The word of the LORD came to me," or "I saw," or "I heard a voice behind me, saying." That word came as "a burden" laid on the prophet, for it was a word of judgment and severe destruction if there was no repentance. There was no resisting that word or its constraints (Jer. 20:9).

Scripture often associates prophecy with music. Not only was music used to soothe King Saul's perturbed spirit, but we are told that whole companies of prophets played musical instruments as they processed down the road (1 Sam. 10:5). When Elisha was not in the proper frame of mind to prophesy, he requested a minstrel to play for him so that he could get on with his work of prophesying

1. Robert B. Girdlestone, *The Grammar of Prophecy: A Systematic Guide to Biblical Prophecy* (Grand Rapids: Kregel, 1955), p. 36.

(2 Kings 3:15). Music, however, could not supply the message of the word. It was not an incantation or anything of the sort. Rather, it had the effect of quieting the disturbed thoughts and attitudes of the prophets, and of setting theology in the context of doxology.

It must also be noted that while the prophetic gift was not hereditary or achievable by any human effort, there did appear schools of the prophets during Samuel's time and during the days of Elijah and Elisha. The pupils or disciples, some of whom were married and short of cash, would gather food for the dining hall or build enlarged facilities in exchange for instruction (2 Kings 4). Their instructor or mentor was called "father" (2 Kings 2:12), and they lived in a common house (2 Kings 6:1–2). According to 2 Kings 4:38, 42–43, approximately one hundred in training at Gilgal took meals together; the number at Jericho was at least fifty (2 Kings 2:7, 16–17). There are no indications of the numbers at Ramah (1 Sam. 19:18–20) or at Bethel (2 Kings 2:3).

The large number of prophets who helped to carry on the ministry of Elijah raises the question of their means of support. Apparently it was not unheard of to offer a gift for services rendered, as Saul did (1 Sam. 9:8). Balak likewise offered a fee to Balaam (Num. 22:7), and Naaman intended to do the same for his cure from leprosy (2 Kings 5:15). Even King Ben-Hadad of Syria sent a gift when he consulted Elisha as to whether he would get up from his sickbed (2 Kings 8:8). The man from Baal Shalishah brought his firstfruits to Elisha (2 Kings 4:42). Thus the prophets were supported by their personal means, fees for some of their services, and offerings of the people.

At the centers of Ramah, Gilgal, Bethel, and Jericho, spiritual instruction was imparted. The pupils also prophesied together, apparently by encouraging, comforting, and strengthening one another, as 1 Corinthians 14:3 suggests. Moreover, they served as spiritual messengers on behalf of the prophets under whom they trained. Elisha

sent one of them to anoint Jehu king of Israel (2 Kings
9:1–3). In another instance, God used one of the "sons of
the prophets" to rebuke King Ahab for his lenient treat-
ment of King Ben-Hadad of Syria (1 Kings 20:35–43). We
see, then, that they played more than just a passive role in
the prophetic ministry of Israel.

The office of prophet was not, as some moderns have
conjectured, a late development to cope with the deficien-
cies of the priesthood and the apostasy of Israel. The Mosaic
law itself provided for the prophetic institution (Deut.
18:15–22). It was that same law which provided the prophets with much of their doctrine. They were preachers of
the law, in the best sense.

Prophecy is more than "fore-telling"; it is mostly "forth-
telling." Less than a third of what the prophets had to say
had to do with the future. Two-thirds of their message was
a setting forth of the word of God against the backdrop of
the failure of the people to obey the moral law of God.
The prophets rebuked vice, idolatry, infidelity (both mar-
ital and spiritual), oppression, iniquity, and corruption at
all levels of society. The essence of their message was,
"Remember the law of my servant Moses, the decrees and
laws I gave him at Horeb for all Israel" (Mal. 4:4). They
were called to "declare to my people their rebellion and to
the house of Jacob their sins" (Isa. 58:1).

Interwoven with this ethical preaching were numerous
predictions of future events, focusing on the Messiah, the
nation Israel, the Gentiles, and the age and kingdom that
were to come. Notice that this focus of the prophets was
not restricted to their own generation and times; rather,
they were given a word that far outstripped such temporal
confinements.

In addition to their continual calls to the nation of Israel
to repent and to heed the word of God, the prophets exercised a surprisingly large ministry to the Gentile nations. Significant portions of their writings are given over
to God's challenge to the heathen dominions to likewise

return to the one true God, to his standards of righteousness and morality. Large sections of the major prophets'
works deal with the Gentiles: Isaiah 13–23; Jeremiah
46–51; Ezekiel 25–32. And there are Amos 1–2, the entire
prophecies of Jonah, Nahum, Obadiah, and many other
sections in the prophets.

But how, one may ask, did the prophets get their messages to these nations? Jeremiah 27:3 informs us that Jeremiah sent messages by means of the ambassadors who
represented their countries in Jerusalem. On another occasion, Jeremiah enlisted a staff officer to carry a message
to Babylon and to read it aloud there (Jer. 51:59–64). Thus
it is clear that these prophecies were more than shadow
boxing or curses uttered in the absence of the affected
party with no expectation of a response on their part. On
the contrary, the calls for the Gentiles to repent were just
as serious as the calls to Israel.

All of this activity seems to have ended with Malachi
in the fifth century B.C. According to 1 Maccabees 4:46;
9:27; and 14:41, no more prophets were sent by God to
the Jewish people during the intertestamental period.
Nevertheless, during that long silent period of four hundred
years between the two Testaments, it was still believed
that prophecy would be revived during the messianic age
even as Joel 2:28 had forecast: "Your sons and your daughters will prophesy." Moreover, God would "send . . . the
prophet Elijah before that great and dreadful day of the
LORD" (Mal. 4:5). Indeed, the Messiah himself would be
a prophet like Moses (Deut. 18:15–19). And that is what
Jesus was acclaimed to be (Matt. 21:11, 46; Luke 7:16;
John 4:19; 9:17); certainly that is what Jesus called himself
(Matt. 13:57; Luke 13:33). He was that prophet who was
to come (Acts 3:22–23; 7:37).

The office of prophet continues in the New Testament
church (1 Cor. 12:28; Eph. 4:11). For example, the prophet
Agabus predicted a coming famine (Acts 11:27–28). Paul
and Barnabas were called to be missionaries through cer-

tain prophets at Antioch (Acts 13:1–3), and Paul's coming afflictions were also predicted by Agabus (Acts 21:10–11). Judas and Silas were prophets in the early church (Acts 15:32), and Timothy received his spiritual gifts through prophecy (1 Tim. 4:14).

The reasons why God set the gift of prophecy in the church are made clear in 1 Corinthians 14: (1) the "strengthening, encouragement and comfort" of the body (v. 3); (2) the instruction of others (vv. 19, 29–31); (3) the conviction of sinners and the convincing of the unlearned (vv. 23–25); and (4) the occasional prediction of future events (Acts 21:10–11).

Once again we note that the New Testament joins the Old in warning against false prophets. Jesus alerted us to their inevitable appearance (Matt. 7:15; 24:11, 24), and Paul warned the elders at Ephesus that they too could expect false prophets to arise after his departure from them (Acts 20:27–31). In John's day they had already arrived (1 John 4:1–3). And in the end day, these leeches and parasites on the true word of God will play a significant role in disturbing the hearts and minds of the church and populace in general (Rev. 16:13; 19:20; 20:10). All of this calls for redoubled vigilance on the part of the church.

For Further Study

Bullock, C. Hassell. "Introduction." In *An Introduction to the Old Testament Prophetic Books*, pp. 11–36. Chicago: Moody, 1986.

Freeman, Hobart E. "Function of the Prophet," and "Cessation of Old Testament Prophecy and Prophecy in the New Testament." In *An Introduction to the Old Testament Prophets*, pp. 37–50, 130–32. Chicago: Moody, 1968.

Mays, James Luther, and Paul J. Achtemeier, eds. *Interpreting the Prophets*, pp. 1–287. Philadelphia: Fortress, 1987. This is a collection of twenty-one essays which originally appeared in five issues of *Interpretation* dating from 1978 to 1985. They should be used with caution since they do not in all instances reflect the positions advocated here.

PART 2

Biblical Theology

7

Develop a Method
for Studying Prophecy

T here is no royal road to the scientific study of prophecy," advised Robert B. Girdlestone. "We have to begin with words and sentences before we launch into ideas."[1] Girdlestone's judgment still stands, even though many claim to have found the royal road. In fact, that may be the reason for so many divisions and such diversity among evangelicals on the subject of the future and the last things: there are too many hucksters of one royal road or another!

There is another issue here as well—the sheer bulk of the prophetic Scriptures. The range of prophecy extends from Genesis to Revelation. It requires a tremendous ability to assemble all the texts on any given subject, digest their meaning, and arrange them in a way that fully integrates all of the predictions in the order of their fulfilment. Such a mastery would require an exhaustive study of all the prophetic literature, unusual ability in the biblical languages, finely honed skills in exegesis, and more than a passing knowledge of the historical, archeological, and literary backgrounds.

1. Robert B. Girdlestone, *The Grammar of Prophecy: A Systematic Guide to Biblical Prophecy* (Grand Rapids: Kregel, 1955), p. 104.

This is not to say that the Bible is not clear, nor that the average reader is unable to interpret prophecy. But it does issue a call for genuine humility, no matter who picks up the text to interpret it. And while we acknowledge the Reformation principle of the priesthood of all believers and the perspicuity or clearness of the message of salvation, this does not mean that everything in the Bible is equally clear, nor that there are no hard things; even the apostle Peter labeled some of Paul's writings "hard to understand" (2 Pet. 3:16). It is a fact that some things are difficult! That is why we need the second principle along with the priesthood of all believers: the appeal to the biblical languages in order to discover the original truth-intention of the author. But even this tool is just that: a tool. It is no guarantee of success nor an open sesame to all the problems encountered in interpreting prophecies. Thus there are no royal roads in the study of prophecy for either the layperson or the scholar. Both will need to begin with words, sentences, and some of the great teaching passages on each topic in biblical prophecy before stepping out to study biblical prophecy at large.

It is imperative, then, that a particular theory not be imposed upon a text before we listen carefully to what that text has to say. The requirements here are a rigorous fidelity to the text of Scripture, a thorough study of its historical and literary context, and an ability to bring together and integrate details which truly contribute to the subject without introducing matters that really belong to other subjects.

Even though the student of prophecy may proceed by tracing certain subjects through the Bible as a whole, it is much safer and wiser to take each of the biblical books, or even each of the main teaching passages on the great subjects of prophecy, and to examine their contents apart from all other considerations. For each of these passages or books where prophetic elements are found, we need to go word by word, sentence by sentence, paragraph by paragraph, until we have a clear idea of what the whole matter is all about. There are several key steps in carrying out this more studied and safer approach:

1. *Determine the relative date of the book or passage under consideration.* It may not always be possible to give an absolute date, such as 520 B.C. for the Book of Haggai, but the interpreter should be able to place the message of the book in a general historical period; for example, Mosaic, premonarchial, Davidic-Solomonic, the Elijah-Elisha era (ca. the ninth century B.C.—Joel, Obadiah), the age of Hezekiah (ca. the eighth century—Jonah, Amos, Hosea, Micah, Isaiah), the age of Josiah (ca. the seventh century—Zephaniah, Habakkuk, Nahum, Jeremiah), the exilic period (the sixth century—Daniel, Ezekiel), and the age of the restoration to the land (the fifth century—Haggai, Zechariah, Malachi).

Determining the general historical period establishes the theater of current events in which the book in question was written. Usually the better the interpreter's understanding of the political machinations and religious trends, the more meaningful will the prophetic text become. God's word is rarely, if ever, disassociated from the historical sphere in which it was first communicated.

Two opposing mistakes are made today in the realm of historical interpretation. Radical criticism wants to limit prophecy to purely historical considerations and thereby to rid it of its supernatural character. Prophecy, however, is more than a historical notice. It links contemporary history with God's plan for the ages.

Reacting conservatism, on the other hand, has observed the deadness and pitifully small yield garnered by the historical research on Scripture. Consequently, a new school of interpreters has arisen which avoids, for the most part, any historical discussions and examines the text without any consideration of its location in time and space. This is like repeating the Apostles' Creed and deleting all historical references such as "suffered under Pontius Pilate" and "the third day he arose." No, prophecy and history belong together. We must be careful of the excesses on either side. History has a part to play, but it must not dominate.

2. *Determine the main divisions of the biblical book and note where the prophetic themes occur in the narrative and logic of the text.* In order to be able to properly identify the message of any book, we need to know how that book was put together. As significant as the seams are in a garment, so are the seams in the development of a book.

The sections of a book may be signaled by a repeated word or phrase such as "this is the account of . . ." ("these are the generations of . . . ," KJV), which occurs ten times in Genesis; "when Jesus had finished [saying these things]," which ends five discourses in Matthew; or "eat and drink and find satisfaction in the work God has given," a rhetorical device appearing four times in Ecclesiastes. In other books the divisions will be less obvious; a change of subject may alert us to the fact that a new section has been initiated. In other cases it will be a change in the person(s) addressed, a change in location, a change in time, or a change in the literary form in which the message is cast.

3. *Identify the different topics, subjects, or themes within each section.* Sometimes these subdivisions of the major sections in each book correspond to the chapter divisions, but this is not an infallible rule (some of the chapters are poorly divided). Once the different topics have been identified, the interpreter must find the focal point for each. The focal point is the key verse, clause, or phrase which most clearly epitomizes what the prophet is saying about that topic.

4. *Determine where to make the paragraph divisions within the subject under investigation.* It is important here that the interpreter consult a number of translations that indicate paragraph divisions along with making his or

her own decision about where the paragraph divisions come in the text.

After the number and exact length of the paragraphs dealing with each subject have been ascertained, the interpreter should attempt to identify the topic sentence of each of these paragraphs. In 95 percent of the cases, a topic sentence will be explicitly stated in the text. It may come at the beginning, the middle, or the end of the paragraph. This exercise will ensure that we will be following the line of thought in the writer's mind rather than a flash of insight that may have suddenly occurred to us the interpreters.

5. *Read the text under investigation in light of its direct citations, allusions, and references to its biblical predecessors.* Even though there are many writers of Scripture spread over an enormous amount of time, the divine message of the Bible is a continuous one. Often God's latest word deliberately builds on what Scripture has previously said on the subject.

We emphasize this principle, which has been called the analogy of antecedent Scripture, because we often miss the milieu in which the discourse was first delivered. Our ears and eyes are not attuned to catching the obvious signals that meant so much to the original speakers and listeners who heard the old themes and phrases ringing through the new revelations from God. It is at this point that most people make their biggest mistake in the interpreting process.

The best way to become sensitive to these types of allusions is to study the marginal references found in many Bibles. The most exhaustive resource that I know of is *The Treasury of the Bible.* But a good chain-reference Bible will supply many of the same references.

6. *Do a word study on the most important terms in the passage.* Usually one need study only two to four significant terms for each separate text under consideration. These will be the terms that have taken on a technical

status because of the history of their usage in Scripture. They may well prove to be the terms that give us the most difficulty when we read the passage, or the terms with which we are not familiar.

In doing a word study, certain questions need to be answered:

1. How many times is the word used in Scripture?
2. In how many different ways is it translated?
3. In how many different types of context is it found?
4. Into what categories may these different usages be grouped?
5. Which usage most adequately reflects the meaning in the text we are interpreting, and how do similar contexts illustrate this usage?

Once these questions are answered, the meanings of the words which have been selected as the most significant terms must be integrated with the themes of each of the paragraphs in which they are found. The contribution of each paragraph to the subject matter at hand can then be set forth.

7. *Summarize what has been learned and relate it to all other biblical teaching on the same subject, especially that which is found in later Scriptures.* A sense of the wholeness of Scripture can be gained from the summaries for each major paragraph and for the whole passage. It must be stressed, however, that any premature interjection of later revelation onto earlier texts is not methodologically defensible. This is more an eisegesis of a passage, not a process of leading the meaning out from the text itself (exegesis).

A cautious use of books on systematic theology or doctrine may be introduced at this point. This will alert us to other contexts of Scripture where the same or similar themes may appear. The claims of these theological reference books should not be automatically accepted, but should be tested in each case.

In addition to these general procedural steps a number of questions may be raised as we consider the details of each passage. A modified list from Girdlestone includes:

1. What part is historic and what is predictive?
2. What functions as figurative drapery and what is real?
3. What sayings are conditional and what is absolute?
4. What parts have been fulfilled since the prophecy was originally given and what remains unfulfilled?
5. What is addressed to Israel directly and what relates to the nations or the church?
6. What is strictly physical and what is spiritual?
7. What is messianic and what is terrestrial?[2]

Some of the issues raised here will be treated in later chapters, while others have already been discussed in our earlier chapters. It is important, however, to see the list as a whole as we approach the interpreting process.

The method we have suggested is the best route for getting at the message of prophecy. It is not an easy course of study, but no one said that it would be. The results, however, are more than worth all the effort.

A second, but strictly subsidiary, approach can now be suggested: the study of the main subjects of prophecy. The best way to proceed is not by collecting all the verses that deal with any given subject; instead, it is to select those passages, usually whole chapters (or a paragraph or two), which either present an entire prophetic scheme in outline (e.g., Dan. 2 and 7) or give to us the fullest explication of a prophetic theme. These chapters may be regarded as the real keys to prophecy.

Because of the richness of Scripture, any list of key passages would probably be defective, but there are some that are so seminal and fundamental to the study of all the other prophetic texts that one would be handicapped not

2. Ibid., pp. 107–8.

to have mastered the content and teaching of these chapters before going on to do exegetical work in new contexts. The following should be mastered prior to any extended study of prophecy:

Genesis 12	The promise made to Abraham
Genesis 49	Jacob's blessing of the twelve tribes
Leviticus 26 and Deuteronomy 28	The alternative prospects of blessing for obedience and judgment for disobedience
2 Samuel 7	The promise of a kingdom to David
Isaiah 9	The promise of Immanuel and his dominion
Isaiah 24	The devastation of the earth and the millennium
Isaiah 52:13–53:12	The Suffering Servant of the Lord
Isaiah 65–66	The new heavens and the new earth
Jeremiah 31:31–34	The promise of the new covenant
Ezekiel 37	The restoration of Israel
Daniel 2 and 7	The succession of empires and the kingdom of God
Joel 2:28–3:21	The coming of the Holy Spirit and the judgment on the nations' final assault against Israel
Amos 9:11–15	The restoration of David's hut
Micah 4	The future assembly of the nations in Jerusalem

Zechariah 14	The second coming of Messiah on the Mount of Olives
Matthew 24–25	Signs of the end of the age and the second coming of Messiah
Romans 9–11	The regrafting of Israel into the olive tree
1 Corinthians 15	The resurrection of the body
2 Corinthians 5:1–10	The intermediate state of the body
Ephesians 2:11–3:11	The mystery of the inclusion of the Gentiles and Jews in one body
2 Thessalonians 2	The disclosure of the Antichrist
Revelation 20:1–10	The millennium
Revelation 21–22	The closing of this age and the introduction of the eternal state

Now all of this is a tall order indeed. But surely each of these passages will be recognized as a major source of the doctrines described. There are other passages that probably should have been included, for example, Daniel 9:24–27 and 1 Thessalonians 4:13–18. But there are more than enough to master in this list. The beginning student would do well just to concentrate on these chapters before attempting any systematic statement on prophecy, the future, and the last things.

One question we have not touched on, but is on the tip of almost everyone's tongue as the subject of studying prophecy is raised: "How literal is the text?" We will reserve our final answer for later (chap. 11). But in the meantime it is important to affirm that the text must be taken naturally, as the writer meant it to be taken. This entails avoiding the extremes of uniform, even wooden, literalism and allegorizing and spiritualizing whenever we encounter a concept which we judge could not be fulfilled naturally in the real world. To adopt a uniform literalism (with which, according to some definitions, we are in sympathy) leaves no room for any figurative expressions, any symbolism or typological usages. No one I know of wishes to be that wooden; all disavow that form of universal literalism.

We must also resist the temptation to try to explain away features of some of the prophecies which seem too fantastic (even when allowance is made for figurative language) for any event in the real world. A good illustration would be Joel's programmatic reference to the moon being turned into blood and the sun into darkness (2:31). To claim that this was fulfilled when our Lord hung on the cross from noon until three in the afternoon might speak to the darkness, but not to the connection between blood and the moon, nor to the contextual associations made by Joel. We are just too quick to make facile equations, for example, between Old Testament Israel and the New Testament church. This is such a significant move that it needs to be backed up with more than a theological declaration.

Even though there are no royal roads in the study of prophecy, there are clear procedures for all who wish to put forth the necessary effort. They will be appropriately rewarded with a grand view of time and eternity. Prophecy is indeed a challenging topic of study and should be undertaken only if one is willing to expend oneself in something more than a manual of quick answers or an everyman's handy chart of the future.

For Further Study

Armerding, Carl E., and W. Ward Gasque, eds. *Dreams, Visions and Oracles: The Layman's Guide to Biblical Prophecy.* Grand Rapids:

Baker, 1977. Sixteen essays by different evangelical writers on interpreting prophecy.

Girdlestone, Robert B. "Methods of Studying Prophecy." In *The Grammar of Prophecy: A Systematic Guide to Biblical Prophecy*, pp. 104–14. Grand Rapids: Kregel, 1955. An excellent outline with an illustration on the structure of the Book of Revelation.

Hasel, Gerhard F. *Understanding the Living Word of God*, pp. 179–234. Mountain View, Calif.: Pacific, 1980. An enjoyable presentation by a leading Adventist theologian.

La Rondelle, Hans K. "Interpretation of Prophetic and Apocalyptic Eschatology." In *A Symposium on Biblical Hermeneutics*, ed. Gordon M. Hyde, pp. 225–49. Washington, D.C.: Review and Herald, 1974. A more strident essay by another Adventist theologian who shares many similarities with evangelical scholars and students.

Pentecost, J. Dwight. *Things to Come: A Study in Biblical Eschatology*. Grand Rapids: Zondervan, 1969. Probably the most useful manual and compendium of eschatological thinking in dispensational circles.

Tan, Paul Lee. *The Interpretation of Prophecy*. Winona Lake, Ind.: BMH, 1974. A strong case for a dispensational hermeneutic; a companion volume to Pentecost.

8

Center on the Promise-Plan of God

The question arises, In the light of all the admitted diversity of materials, plurality of themes, and multiplicity of forms in the Old and New Testaments, how is our study of prophecy to proceed? Since "the testimony of Jesus is the spirit of prophecy" (Rev. 19:10), it is obviously as unthinkable to study prophecy without reference to Jesus as it is to study the body without reference to the head. The Messiah is the central focus of all prophecy. To the objection of the majority of today's Bible scholars that the decision to focus on the Messiah is a choice made from outside the texts and not derived from within, we respond that the Bible revolves around the person of the Messiah. It begins with a promise in Genesis 3:15, "He [the Seed of the woman] will crush your [the serpent's, i.e., the devil's] head," and ends with the same focus in Revelation 22:20, "Yes, I am coming soon." Between these two great bookends lies the story of God's great accomplishment of this one promise-plan.

Our English word *promise* means "a declaration or assurance made to another person with respect to the future, stating that one will do, or refrain from, some specific act, or that one will give or bestow some specific thing, usually in a good sense, implying something to the advantage or pleasure of the person concerned" (*Oxford English Dictionary*). Our use of this word to embody all that God was and is going to do for the human race reflects the New Testament's repeated use of the term to refer back to the Old Testament pledges of God. The Old Testament embodies the same concept through a constellation of terms: God's "word," "oath," "blessing," and the like.

The New Testament uses both the noun *promise* (52 times; 26 times in Paul, 14 times in Hebrews, 9 times in Luke, twice in 2 Peter, once in 1 John) and the verb *to promise* (15 times; 5 times in Paul, 4 in Hebrews, twice in James, and once each in Mark, Acts, 2 Peter, and 1 John). Thus the word *promise* is used by every New Testament author except Matthew and Jude. Listing all of these New Testament references is only by way of forming a hypothesis which needs to be tested by actual exegesis as outlined in the previous chapter. But before we turn to the actual progress of the doctrine and attempt to demonstrate the march of the promise-plan through the Bible, let it be noted that "promise" can denote either the form in which the words appear or their content. Thus "promise" may refer either to the declaration itself as worthy of confidence or to the items which are pledged. Since God's one promise-plan has a number of specifications, the plural form *promises* appears twelve times in the New Testament. The singular form, however, is the overwhelming preference, for the New Testament writers viewed the whole collection as an integrated totality and as a single plan.

The promise of God begins with his declaration to do something which will benefit the whole human race. At the heart of the promise are the gifts that God will bestow on a few in order to benefit the many. Therefore, in tracing this theme throughout both Testaments we will define the promise as the divine declaration or assurance given at first to Adam and Eve, Shem, Abraham, Isaac, and Jacob, and then to the whole nation of Israel, that (1) he would be their God, (2) they would be his people, and (3) he would dwell in the midst of his people. By means of the family and nation he had chosen to be his instrument, God would bring the same gifts and works to all the peoples of the earth.

The great historical series of promises constitutes one of the most significant sets of prophecies in all of the Bible. It was through this channel that God disclosed his great plan of salvation for humanity and his plan for the ages. A brief outline of that development should help us to appreciate its centrality.

1. *The blessing of the prepatriarchal era (Gen. 1–11).* At first the promise of God was simply called his blessing. It included God's gift of the creation and his three declarations following the three great crises of the fall, the flood, and the fiasco at the tower of Babel.

In Genesis 3:15 God promised to remedy the entrance of sin into the world by guaranteeing that the Seed (i.e., a future descendant) of the woman would strike a decisive blow against the serpent, while the serpent in turn would be able only to briefly wound his heel. After sin had brought on the flood, there came a new word: God himself would dwell in the tents of Shem (Gen. 9:27 KJV). That is to say, the blessing of the seed would be transmitted through the Semitic people. Similarly, after the tower of Babel, the third major crisis on planet earth, a new addition to the promise came: one Semite named Abraham would be the medium through which God would perpetuate this blessing and transmit it to all the nations of the earth who would believe and accept it (Gen. 12:1–3).

2. *The trifold promise given to the patriarchs—Abraham, Isaac, and Jacob (Gen. 12–50).* The first provision of the promise to Abraham involved land. After he had journeyed from the city of Ur in Babylonia, he came to Shechem, in the plain of Moreh, where the Lord appeared to him and said, "To your offspring I will give this land" (Gen. 12:7). Some twenty years later, when he was ninety-

nine years old, the boundaries of this land were described
to him. It would extend from the river of Egypt (Wadi el-
Arish) in the southwest to the great river Euphrates on
the northeast (Gen. 15:18; see also Gen. 12:1, 7; 13:17;
17:8; 24:7; 26:3–5; 28:13, 15; 35:12; 48:4; 50:24). This
land would be part of an everlasting covenant that contained two other key provisions.

The second provision was the promise of a seed. The
important point to observe here is that the word *seed* is
neither a singular nor a plural noun, but a singular collective. As such, it deliberately included all the offspring of
the patriarch as well as the representative individual who
epitomized the whole group. This individual is the same
one who had been promised ages ago to Adam and Eve in
Genesis 3:15, and who would, in the progress of revelation,
be disclosed as none other than the Messiah himself. References to this heir are numerous in Genesis 12–50 (12:7;
15:4; 21:12; 22:16–18; 26:3–4, 24; 28:13–14; 35:11–12).

The third part of this promise was that in Abraham's
seed all the nations of the earth would be blessed (Gen.
12:3). It was this portion of the promise that the apostle
Paul referred to as the gospel which had been pre-
announced to Abraham—the same gospel, mind you, that
Paul was preaching! Indeed, that is how Peter preached
just outside the temple after healing the crippled beggar,
"All the prophets . . . have foretold these days. And you are
heirs of the prophets and of the covenant God made with
your fathers. He said to Abraham, 'Through your offspring
all peoples on earth will be blessed' " (Acts 3:24–25). This
promise of the gospel was repeated five times to the fathers
(Gen. 12:3; 18:18; 22:17–18; 26:4; 28:14).

To show the eternality and one-sidedness of the obligation to maintain this trifold promise, only God passed
between the pieces of the animals which Abraham had
cut in two (Gen. 15:9–21). God thereby obliged himself to
fulfil these promises without simultaneously requiring
Abraham and subsequent beneficiaries to take an oath.

3. *The promise-plan and the works of the law.* The promise could not be withdrawn by mortals or God; it was an everlasting word. Fail as men and women would, the promise would still be transmitted through the generations until Christ emerged from the predicted line. The reception of the gift was not automatic, however; in order to participate in this gift, individuals had to believe in the Man of promise who was to come (Gen. 15:6).

Where faith was already present prior to the Sinai legislation, obedience to the demands and commands of God's law was the natural outcome. Therefore, Abraham is said to have walked blamelessly before God (Gen. 17:1) and to have obeyed God's requirements, commands, decrees, and laws (Gen. 26:5).

The law extended God's demands from faith to the entire life of the people. The earlier promises were the basis on which such demands could be made (see Exod. 2:23–25; 6:2–8; 19:3–8; 20:2). Far from nullifying the law either for Israel or for Paul (Rom. 3:31), the promises of God were actually its foundation.

4. *The promise to David of a kingdom, a throne, and a dynasty.* In spite of all the laws, institutions, and hopes for the present and the future, the only surety for Israel and the world rested in the word of God. Even the institution of the monarchy, prematurely founded on the whims of the people, who desired to be like the other nations in having a king to lead them, was given a distinctive role in the promise of God. He took a lad "from the pasture" (2 Sam. 7:8) and made his "name great, like the names of the greatest men of the earth" (2 Sam. 7:9). What is more, his seed would be seated at the right hand of God (Ps. 110:1) and inherit the nations (Ps. 2:8) as his realm.

So startled was David by God's surprise announcement through Nathan the prophet that he would be given an everlasting dynasty, throne, and kingdom (2 Sam. 7:16) that he could not begin to express his delight and confused joy. But what really shocked him was the fact that what he had just been promised was in direct line with the earlier word that had been given to Adam and Eve and to the patriarchs. Moreover, this promise was "the charter for [all] humanity" (2 Sam. 7:19, my own translation). The ancient promise, which had been the object of David's faith and the divinely ordained means by which all the nations of the earth would be blessed, was now being invested in his seed, his house, his throne, his kingdom! He could hardly believe what he was hearing!

5. *The gift of the Holy Spirit promised through the prophet Isaiah.* The action of the Holy Spirit on the inner person is a topic which is mentioned infrequently, but surely, in the Old Testament. The Spirit whom Isaiah promises on several occasions is clearly the Spirit of promise referred to in Luke 24:49; John 15:26; Acts 1:4; and Ephesians 1:13.

For example, Isaiah 32:15 depicts the Spirit's arrival as a first step to the reign of righteousness, for "till the Spirit is poured upon us from on high, and the desert becomes a fertile field," justice, righteousness, peace, quietness, and confidence will not be completely in charge of all of life. God promises, "I will pour water on the thirsty land. . . . I will pour out my Spirit on your offspring, and my blessing on your descendants" (Isa. 44:3). Here his promised blessing is a downpour, a veritable tropical cloudburst, of his Holy Spirit on his own. These words are very reminiscent of our Lord's conversation with Nicodemus in John 3:5 and of Jesus' promise in John 7:38–39, " 'Whoever believes in me, as the Scripture has said, streams of living water will flow from within him.' By this he meant the Spirit, whom those who believed in him were later to receive." This was God's cure for thirsty souls in the Old and New Testaments. Joel (2:28–29), of course, had predicted this same deluge of the Holy Spirit in abundant fashion. And Peter later affirmed that what was happening on the day of Pentecost was indeed that which had been promised by the prophet Joel.

In Isaiah 59:19–21 the gift of the Holy Spirit is connected with the new covenant. The prophet sees individuals coming from the east and west, driven by the Spirit of the Lord, to their Redeemer in Zion. " 'As for me, this is my [new] covenant with them,' says the LORD. 'My Spirit, who is in you, and my words that I have put in your mouth will not depart from your mouth, or from the mouths of your children, or from the mouths of their descendants from this time on and forever,' says the Lord" (v. 21). Just as God's words have already been given, at least in some measure, so his Holy Spirit has likewise been distributed to all his children who believe.

Similarly, Isaiah 61:1 declares that the Holy Spirit will anoint the coming Messiah for the tasks which he must perform as the Servant of the Lord. From this anointing by the Spirit will flow all his blessings on both Jews and Gentiles. No wonder, then, that 1 John 2:27 declares, "As his anointing teaches you about all things and as that anointing is real, not counterfeit . . . [you ought to] remain in him."

The fact that Joel stressed that this downpour of the Holy Spirit would be upon "all people" clearly indicates that the original objective of the blessing and the inclusion of the Gentiles in the Abrahamic promise (Gen. 12:3) had not been lost over the centuries. It would include those "who are far off" (Acts 2:39), an obvious circumlocution or roundabout way of saying "Gentiles" without actually using that pejorative term (cf. the use of phrases like "all mankind" in Gen. 6:12–13; Num. 16:22; Ps. 65:2; Isa. 40:5–6; Jer. 32:27; etc.).

6. *The promise of the new covenant to Jeremiah.* While the new covenant repeats many of the elements and formulas contained in the previously announced promise-plan of God, it also adds some key new features. For example, it repeats that God will be the God of those whom he has chosen, and they will be his people, and he will forgive them of their sin. Yes, and the law which God gave

to Moses will still be in force. But now that law will be
internalized and written on the hearts of God's people instead of just being inscribed on stone. No longer, promises
Jeremiah, will it be necessary to teach one's neighbors or
brother, for everyone will know the Lord. That surely will
be new! Jeremiah 31:31–34 certainly is one of the great
highlights of the Old Testament.

Though Israel will lose its king, its capital, its temple,
and its glory, God will still fulfil the ancient promises. He
will provide a new David (our Lord Jesus), a new temple,
a new Elijah (John the Baptist and one of the two witnesses
of Rev. 11), and new heavens and a new earth—all in fulfilment of what he pledged long ago!

7. *The New Testament's continuation and enlarge-
ment of the ancient promise of God.* Almost every New
Testament use of the word *promise (epangelia)* points back
to the Old Testament. The following list will give some
idea of the wide variety of specifications within the single
promise:

> The promises given to Abraham—Acts 7:17; Romans
> 4:13, 14, 16, 20, 21; 9:8, 9; Galatians 3:14, 16, 17, 18,
> 19, 21, 22, 29; 4:23, 28; Hebrews 6:12, 13, 15, 17; 7:6;
> 9:15; 10:23; 11:9, 11, 13, 17
>
> The promises given to all three patriarchs and David—
> Acts 26:6; Romans 15:8
>
> The promises given to Moses—2 Corinthians 7:1; Ephe-
> sians 6:2; Hebrews 4:1
>
> The promises given to David—Acts 13:23; 2 Corinthians
> 7:1
>
> The promises given to the prophets—Romans 1:2
>
> The promise that the Gentiles will partake of the bless-
> ings of the gospel—Galatians 3:8, 14, 29
>
> The promise of the resurrection from the dead—Acts
> 26:6–8; 2 Timothy 1:1; Hebrews 9:15; 10:36; 2 Peter
> 3:4, 9; 1 John 2:25

The promise of the Holy Spirit in a new fulness—Luke
24:49; Acts 1:4; 2:33, 39; Galatians 3:14

The promise of redemption from sin—Romans 4:2–5,
9–10; James 2:21–23

The promise of the Messiah—Acts 13:23; Gal. 3:22

Even though there were so many promises, they were
treated as one single promise. Accordingly, when Paul had
to defend himself before Agrippa, he concluded, "And now
it is because of my hope in what God has promised our
fathers that I am on trial today. This is the promise our
twelve tribes are hoping to see fulfilled as they earnestly
serve God day and night" (Acts 26:6–7). This promise,
then, is central to both the Old and New Testaments.

God has one plan from the beginning to the end: to
benefit one man and through that one man, his family,
and eventually his whole nation, to bless the whole world.
This one promise, the climax of which is the two advents
of Jesus of Nazareth, was continually fulfilled in the Old
and New Testaments. We who believe share in this same
promise.

Surely the promise-plan of God is the centerpiece in the
whole scheme of prophecy and in the total corpus of Scripture. While much of the promise doctrine is prophetic and
therefore often relates to God's future acts, there are notable differences between promise and prophecy. Promises
always relate to what is good and desirable, to that which
blesses and enriches; prophecy may also contain notes of
judgment, calamity, and destruction when individuals and
nations fail to repent. Promises ordinarily implicate the
whole human race in their provisions, while prophecies
typically are aimed at specific cultures, peoples, or individuals. Promises are continuously fulfilled generation after
generation, whereas prophecies speak of the distant future.
Accordingly, Israel is the land of promise (Heb. 11:9), not
the land of prophecy. The promise of God is also unconditional, but most prophecies are conditional, containing

a suppressed "unless" or "if you do not repent." Finally,
the promise of God embraces many general declarations
from God ("great and precious promises," 2 Pet.
1:4), whereas prophecies are usually directed to specific events
and to particular individuals.

Should it be objected that the central theme of the Bible
and its prophetic mission is actually the announcement of
the kingdom and its coming king, the Messiah, Willis J.
Beecher has given a most satisfying response: "But it is on
the basis of the divine promise that [the New Testament]
preachers proclaim the kingdom, and when they appeal to
the Old Testament in proof of Christian doctrine, they
make the promise more prominent than the kingdom itself."[1] Thus the major focus of Scripture is the promise-
plan of God, the unfolding of his purpose to communicate
a blessing to Israel through his person and his works, and
thereby to bless all the nations of the earth.

For Further Study

Beecher, Willis J. "The Promise-Doctrine as Taught in the New Tes-
    tament." In *The Prophets and the Promise,* pp. 175–94. New York:
    Crowell, 1905; Grand Rapids: Baker, 1963.

Blythin, Islwyn. "The Patriarchs and the Promise." *Scottish Journal
    of Theology* 21 (1968): 56–73.

Clines, David J. A. "Formulations: The Patriarchal Promise." In
    The Theme of the Pentateuch, pp. 31–43. Sheffield, England: Uni-
    versity of Sheffield, 1978.

Kaiser, Walter C., Jr. "The Old Testament as the Promise-Plan of God,"
    and "The Old Testament as a Messianic Primer." In *Toward Redis-
    covering the Old Testament,* pp. 83–100, 101–20. Grand Rapids:
    Zondervan, 1987.

McCurley, Foster R., Jr. "The Christian and the Old Testament Prom-
    ise." *Lutheran Quarterly* 22 (1970): 401–10.

————— . "Promise and Fulfillment as Hermeneutical Categories."

    1. Willis J. Beecher, *The Prophets and the Promise* (New York: Crowell,
1905; Grand Rapids: Baker, 1963), pp. 178–79.

In *Proclaiming the Promise: Christian Preaching from the Old Testament,* pp. 29–44. Philadelphia: Fortress, 1974.

Smith, Wilbur M. "Promise." In *Evangelical Dictionary of Theology,* ed. Walter A. Elwell, pp. 885–86. Grand Rapids: Baker, 1984.

9

Check Your Program If You Want to Know Who the Players Are

T he two teams who will play the championship game (well, at least participate in the finale) are Israel and the Gentile nations of the world. What a matchup that will be! But this is jumping far ahead of our story.

The basic issue here is the identity of the people of God. Does Scripture point to the existence of two separate peoples, the nation Israel and the church, or does it see them as some type of whole? Or to put the matter another way, how much continuity and how much discontinuity are there between the discussion of Israel in the Old Testament and the church in the New Testament?

Let us take the Old Testament first and see what term designated Israel as a group having some relationship to God. While the Hebrew words *gôy* and *'am* were both originally used to indicate a group of persons who formed a community, the term *'am* ("people") became the specialized word designating the people of God. *Gôy*, especially in the plural (*gôyim*, "nations"), was reserved for the peoples of foreign lands and for the pagans (Num. 23:9).

The specialized use of *'am* shows that there was a need

for some definite term to express the distinctive nature of
Israel, a people different from the others because of her
divine calling for a distinctive task in the world—a task
which would have an impact on all the nations of the
earth. Israel existed as a nation because God chose them
(Deut. 7:7; Isa. 41:8) and called them (Isa. 48:12), not because they were the most populous race on earth, nor because they would be the most faithful or most meritorious
(Deut. 7:7; 8:17–18; 9:4). It was simply a matter of the
gracious, unmerited favor of God which he embodied in
an everlasting covenant.

Thus far interpreters are fairly much in agreement with
each other. The fur begins to fly when the next question
is asked: Does the "everlasting covenant" that God made
with Abraham in Genesis 17:7–8 mean that Israel still
has a future as a nation? Will Israel yet enjoy all the promises made to her by so many of the prophets, or will she
continue only as a race but not as a nation?

Everyone knows by now that a most extraordinary event
took place in May of 1948. A political state bearing the
name Israel was formed in the Middle East; it had direct
continuity with the people of the Old Testament. No nation has ever been defunct for almost two-and-a-half mil-
lennia, as Israel was from 587 B.C. to A.D. 1948, and
returned to assume her national existence. If this is not
what the prophets were predicting in the Old Testament,
then these forty years of Israel's revived fortunes at least
point the way as to how the prediction might be fulfilled
in the future. But the longer this state continues, the more
likely it is that we are seeing the fulfilment.

In addition to the strong promises repeatedly made to
the patriarchs in passages such as Genesis 15:18–21 and
17:7–8, most pointed pronouncements were later made
concerning the perpetuity of Israel as a nation. One of the
most famous appears right after the promise of the new
covenant in Jeremiah 31:31–34. There God declares that
only if he breaks his covenant with the sun, moon, and

stars, will he break his covenant with the descendants of Israel, so that they cease being a nation! The way I teach this text is to ask the class to look out the windows and tell me if the sun is still shining by day, and the moon and stars are shining in the night. If they say that the heavenly lights are still shining, I assure them that God's oath with Israel *as a nation* is still in force!

Let's look closely at Jeremiah 31:35–37:

> This is what the LORD says, he who appoints the sun to shine by day, who decrees the moon and stars to shine by night, who stirs up the sea so that its waves roar—the LORD Almighty is his name: "Only if these decrees vanish from my sight," declares the LORD, "will the descendants of Israel ever cease to be a nation before me." This is what the LORD says: "Only if the heavens above can be measured and the foundations of the earth below be searched out will I reject all the descendants of Israel because of all they have done," declares the LORD.

Some interpreters have tried to deny the force of this by viewing its promises as conditional on Israel's obedience and consequently as set aside in light of their infamous disobedience. But let it be noted that this extremely strong prophecy of Israel's continuance comes in the context of Israel's most celebrated apostasy, for which she is about to be carried off into captivity.

We have already observed that while most prophecy has a suppressed "unless you repent," the promises made with Abraham, Isaac, Jacob, and David do not fall in this class, for only God was obligated to carry out their provisions. Had Abraham been asked to walk between the pieces of the animals he had cut in two (Gen. 15:9–21), the argument for conditionality might have a leg to stand on; but in fact, he was not invited to do so. There is no "if" or "unless" to argue from! Hence, while a covenant necessarily implies two or more parties, it is possible that because of special circumstances the stipulations may be

110

binding on only one of the parties. That is exactly what happened in Genesis 15. The Lord alone passed between the pieces, and so he alone contracted the obligation.

What then shall we do with the conditional elements that appear to be attached to the Abrahamic promise, such as those in Genesis 12:1–3; 17:1–2, 9–14; 22:15–18; and 26:4–5? We have argued in detail elsewhere that all of the alleged conditions were attached not to the promise, but only to the addressees' participation in what was certain and without reservation from God's perspective and provision.[1] Therefore, many in the line of David who did not personally believe in the coming Messiah, and who thus were not beneficiaries of the promise, were nevertheless transmitters of the messianic line down to the coming of Christ! Through gross disobedience individuals, or a generation, could deprive themselves of the immediate blessings of the promise, but the covenant of God would still have its complete fulfilment.

In what sense was the covenant of Abraham everlasting? Three times we are told in Genesis 17 (vv. 7, 13, 19) that the promise to Abraham was "an everlasting covenant," and that included the land as well. In verse 8 God vows, "The whole land of Canaan, where you are now an alien, I will give as an everlasting possession to you and your descendants after you; and I will be their God." According to its usage in Scripture, "everlasting" refers to the indefinite continuance of the specified object into the future, thus conveying the idea of endlessness. This idea of endlessness can be qualified only by the direct word of God or by the physical nature of the object to which the idea is applied (all physical things must, as a part of heaven and earth, come under the judgment of being laid bare by the fiery work of God in the end times).[2] Given this sure word

1. Walter C. Kaiser, Jr., *Toward an Old Testament Theology* (Grand Rapids: Zondervan, 1978), pp. 92–94.

2. See Robert B. Girdlestone, *Synonyms of the Old Testament* (Grand Rapids: Eerdmans, 1974), p. 317; *Theological Wordbook of the Old Testament*, ed. R. Laird Harris (Chicago: Moody, 1980), vol. 2, p. 672.

of God and the fact that the present heavens and earth are the heavens and earth of the creation, it is clear that the everlasting nature of the promise of the land rules out any possibility that the promise has already been exhaustively fulfilled.

Attempts to tone down the forcefulness of the argument for an everlasting possession of the land have not been successful. It is pointed out, for example, that the word *everlasting* may signify permanence (as in Deut. 15:17) or a distant time (as in Eccles. 1:10) as well as eternity (Ps. 90:2; Dan. 12:2). But what is the difference? The point remains the same: the promise remains in force despite the antics and failures of persons. Only God can say when the end of permanence or a distant time has been reached.

Oftentimes students of the Bible point to three passages that appear to suggest that the promise of land to Israel has indeed been fulfilled: Joshua 21:43–45; 23:14–15; Nehemiah 9:8. These texts assert that "not one of all the LORD's good promises to the house of Israel failed; every one was fulfilled" (Josh. 21:45; cf. 23:14).

However, the boundaries mentioned in Numbers 34:2–12 are not the ones reached in the accounts of Joshua and Judges. For example, Joshua 13:1–7 and Judges 3:1–4 agree in maintaining that there was much land that remained to be taken.

Others point to the land taken by David and Solomon as fulfilling the promise made to the patriarchs and others in such passages as Genesis 15:18; Exodus 23:31; Numbers 13:1–2, 21; 34:1–12; Deuteronomy 11:24; Joshua 15:1–12; 2 Kings 14:25; Isaiah 27:12; and Ezekiel 47:15–20. While 1 Kings 8:65 appears to come close ("from Lebo Hamath to the Wadi of Egypt"), the Solomonic administrative districts do not fully correspond with the promised boundaries. Philistia was not included (1 Kings 4:7–19, 21; 2 Chron. 9:26). That area was only under tribute, not under the direct rule of Israel. A similar situation appears to be the case in the Phoenician coastal area above Tyre, where the Sidonians, for example, never came under either Israelite rule or tribute.

We can only conclude that Israel never fully realized what had been given to her as an everlasting promise.

The statement that "not one of all the LORD's good promises . . . failed" refers to the fact that the process whereby the ultimate fulfilment is going to come already started during Abraham's and Joshua's day. They truly realized a portion of the total work that God is to do in the final day, but in no case could they claim that they had seen the entire work. The emphasis was on the fact that God's promised word had not failed, nor would it. Interpreters of the Scripture must be careful to avoid the tendency of Western dualism to focus on the spiritual side and depreciate the material or physical side of our Lord's triumph in the final days of earth's history.

Having warned about an overemphasis on a dualism which spiritualizes the entire message, we must also state that as the people of God Jews and Gentiles (i.e., Old Testament believers and New Testament believers) are one and not two separate bodies and constituencies. The titles used in the Old Testament to describe mainly Jewish believers are used in the New Testament to describe those who come into the body of Christ through the new birth. In fact, the old three-part formula that had been used to describe the promise-plan and covenant of God with the patriarchs and David in the Old Testament is repeated in the New Testament with regard to the believing church: "You will be my people, I will be your God, and I will dwell in the midst of you" (see 2 Cor. 6:16; Heb. 8:10; Rev. 21:3). The New Testament believers are described as "a people that are his very own" (Titus 2:14; cf. "my treasured possession" in Exod. 19:5), "a chosen people, a royal priesthood, a holy nation, a people belonging to God" (1 Pet. 2:9; cf. Exod. 19:5). Formerly "not my people" and denied mercy, New Testament believers are now identified as "the people of God" and as recipients of his mercy (1 Pet. 2:10; cf. Hos. 1:10; 2:23).

New Testament believers, like Old Testament believers,

are bound to God by his new covenant. The provisions that Jeremiah 31:31–34 offered to Israel are repeated in Hebrews 8 and 10, the most extensive Old Testament quotation to be found in the New Testament. The only conclusion possible is that there is only one people of God even though we can, in view of God's promises to Israel and God's promises to all believers, distinguish two aspects of that one people.

How do these two groups of players, who potentially (if not actually) share so much, fit into the present and final drama of history? The ideal place to go in the New Testament is Romans 9–11. Paul makes two exceedingly important assertions in Romans 11:11–12:

1. Israel's disobedience and consequent scattering were not the end of her calling. She remains the link between the Messiah and the nations—even in her disobedience! As verse 11 contends, "because of their transgression, salvation has come to the Gentiles."
2. If, as a result of Israel's failure, salvation has been extended to so many in the Gentile realm, how much more will the full inclusion of Israel mean, not only for Israel, but for the whole world (v. 12)!

We are reminded that "God's gifts and his call are irrevocable" (Rom. 11:29). What he promised when he passed between the pieces (Gen. 15:9–21) was unilateral and unconditional in its provision for Israel, and thereby for all the world.

According to the plan and by the permission of God, "Israel has experienced a hardening in part *until the full number of the Gentiles has come in*" (Rom. 11:25, italics added). But when the task of evangelizing the pagan, non-Jewish world has been completed and the "full number" of Gentiles have come to believe in Christ, then the time will come for the Jews to experience their "fullness" in God's gracious offer of salvation (Rom. 11:12).

The same timetable can be seen in Jesus' prediction that "Jerusalem will be trodden down by the Gentiles, until the times of the Gentiles are fulfilled" (Luke 21:24 RSV). Unfortunately, this timetable is not a matter of evangelical consensus. Some object in the strongest possible terms to interpreting the first clause in Romans 11:26 in a temporal sense—"And then all Israel will be saved." They prefer to interpret it, "And thus [so, in this manner] all Israel will be saved." Verses 25–26a would then read, "Israel has experienced a hardening in part until the full number of the Gentiles has come in, and *in this way* all Israel will be saved."

The most important point that needs to be raised here is that Romans 11:26b–27 consists of quotations from Isaiah 59:20–21 and Jeremiah 31:33–34. In their Old Testament setting, these verses applied to God's new covenant and to his restoration of Israel. Moreover, in Romans 11:28 ("As far as the gospel is concerned, they are enemies on your account; but as far as election is concerned, they are loved on account of the patriarchs") Israel's future and the extension of salvation to the church are tied in with the ancient promise-plan of God offered first to the patriarchs.

Even though the first clause of Romans 11:26 ("And so all Israel will be saved") may not be directly temporal, it is sequential and consequential in thought in that the promises made in the Abrahamic–Davidic–new covenant are tied to the coming in of the full number of Israel and the Gentiles.

When will this full inclusion of Israel be sequenced into the present operation of God's plan? Some refuse to place this event as late as the end times, but Romans 11:15 does not give them much ground to stand on. Said Paul, "For if their rejection is the reconciliation of the world [i.e., the coming to salvation of the full number of the Gentiles], what will their acceptance [by God] be but life from the dead?"

Now the phrase "life from the dead" could be taken in

a spiritual sense. But this is the very figure that the prophet Ezekiel used to mark the reestablishment of the Jewish people in the land of Israel: "O my people, I am going to open your graves and bring you up from them; I will bring you back to the land of Israel. . . . I will put my Spirit in you and you will live, and I will settle you in your own land" (Ezek. 37:12, 14).

The reference to the "redeemer" or "deliverer [who] will come from Zion" (Rom. 11:26) points to our Lord's *second* coming, not his first coming, as so many have incorrectly attempted to interpret this text. But these interpreters are not wrong that both the Jews and the Gentiles are embraced by one and the same promise-plan of God. After all, the heart of the New Testament message is found in the new covenant of Jeremiah 31:31–34. What is most significant here is that in that very context God pledged to restore Israel to her land once more!

We conclude that there is one people of God in a single program of his ongoing promise-plan; nevertheless, we can distinguish aspects of that one people and that one plan. All who believe in the Man of promise who was to come and who has now come as the Messiah are part of the "people of God"; this term is a strong link between the Testaments. Furthermore, when "the full number of the Gentiles has come in" (or, to use our Lord's words, when "the times of the Gentiles are fulfilled"), then Israel, as a people, will be saved and will finally experience the ultimate enjoyment of the land reaching to the full extent of the boundaries promised in the Torah.

For Further Study

Berkhof, Hendrikus. "The Future Sign—Israel's Conversion." In *Christ the Meaning of History*, trans. Lambertus Buurman, pp. 135–52. Richmond: Knox, 1966.

Kaiser, Walter C., Jr. "The Promised Land: A Biblical-Historical View." *Bibliotheca Sacra* 138 (1981): 302–12.

————— . "Must the Christian Include Israel and Her Land in a Contemporary Theology?" In *Toward Rediscovering the Old Testament,* pp. 46–58. Grand Rapids: Zondervan, 1987.

Townsend, Jeffrey. "Fulfillment of the Land Promise in the Old Testament." *Bibliotheca Sacra* 142 (1985): 320–37.

Contrary Views

MacInnis, John Murdoch. "Israel—The Fulfillment of the Promise." *Biblical Review* 15 (1930): 59–78.

Wilch, John R. "The Land and State of Israel in Prophecy and Fulfillment." *Concordia Journal* 8 (1982): 172–78.

10

Acquaint Yourself with Some of the Basic Plays of the Game

If something big is about to happen in the eternal plan of God, the first thing Westerners want to know is "when?" and "how?" For Euro-Americans the major issue is timing; the details are strictly secondary.

To some degree, the Scriptures satisfy our curiosity by supplying us with the framework of the coming events in God's dramatic conclusion to history and his introduction of eternity itself. But we must avoid any form of date setting or sensationalism. That was never the purpose God intended when he gave us a view of the future. Instead, his purpose was to assure us that he knows where history is going and to convince us to live in such a way that if he should appear suddenly, we would have no need for excuse or embarrassment.

In order to designate the sensational drama which is to come in the last days of history as we know it, the New Testament took over the term and concept of "the day of the Lord" from the Old Testament (e.g., in Acts 2:20 [from Joel 2:31]; 2 Tim. 1:12, 18; 4:8, etc.). Leading up to that hour or day are the two ages mentioned some thirty times in the New Testament.

With the use of the twin terms, "this age" and "the age to come," the New Testament lays down one of the most helpful frameworks from which to view the grand spectacle of God's dramatic conclusion to the series of events that are already in motion. For example, in Mark 10:30 Jesus promises that those who have left all in order to serve him and to spread the gospel will receive a hundred times as much, both "in this present age" and "in the age to come." In Luke 20:34–35 Jesus points out that while people marry in "this age," those worthy of participating "in that age" and in the resurrection from the dead will not marry.

This present age began with creation and will extend in full force up to the second coming of Christ, and then beyond that in a limited fashion for the duration of the millennium, concluding there at the end of history and at the great white judgment throne of Christ (see fig. 1). The age to come, on the other hand, began in a limited form when our Lord cast out demons by the power of God. Then it was that the kingdom of God had come (Matt. 12:28) and we began to taste of the powers of the age to come (Heb. 6:5); indeed, we are now in the "last days" (Heb. 1:2).

In addition to the two ages, the three resurrections Scripture points to also make up a most reliable framework for viewing all of the events in God's future plan. The primary text in this regard is 1 Corinthians 15:22–26:

For as in Adam all die, so in Christ all will be made alive. But each in his own turn: Christ, the firstfruits; then, when

Figure 1 **The Two Ages**

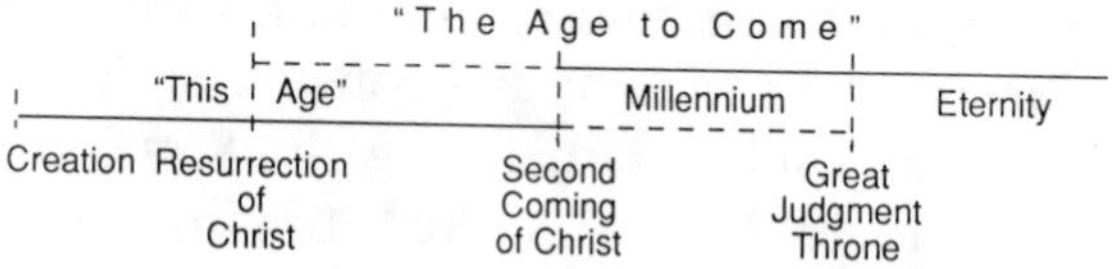

he comes, those who belong to him. Then the end will come, when he hands over the kingdom to God the Father after he has destroyed all dominion, authority and power. For he must reign until he has put all enemies under his feet. The last enemy to be destroyed is death.

It has been incorrectly argued (by Karl Barth and others) that the first sentence in this passage teaches universalism, that everyone is going to be saved and receive eternal life. But where does the emphasis fall? When I was a boy, I used to hear preachers make their voices shake and waver as they told their people that "in Adam *all* die." But when they came to the second half of the sentence, they did not orally italicize the word *all* ("in Christ *all* will be made alive"). Instead, they shouted *"in Christ,"* and then went as fast as they could with their voices trailing away, "all-will-be-made-alive."

Both *alls*, however, should be stressed. This does not lead to universalism! The text simply claims that everyone since Adam has died (the cemetery is proof) and will be resurrected by the power of Christ. It makes no assertions about salvation. Most significant is the fact that the next verse begins with a "But"! I would urge that the period after "alive" be replaced by a comma or a semicolon. (Incidentally, the original Greek text had no punctuation.) The flow of ideas would be: "As in Adam all die, so in Christ all will be made alive; *but* each [one will be resurrected] in his own turn." Thus, while everyone is coming back again, not all are going to experience the joy of living with Christ forever.

The Greek word translated "turn" is a military term. There are three resurrection divisions, platoons, or companies: (1) Christ's resurrection on Easter Sunday morning is the guarantee of the others, the firstfruits of the harvest that is to come; (2) all of the dead who in life received Jesus as Lord and Savior will be raised from their graves, and all surviving believers will at the same time be taken up from the earth to meet him in the air; (3) then comes "the end." But what is this? We believe that it is the resurrection of those who refused to bow their knees and heart in recognition of the King of Kings and Lord of Lords. In other words, this group will be raised at the end of the millennium to appear before the great white judgment throne and be asked why they never received Jesus as their personal Savior. Notice that at that time everything will be turned over to God the Father, and every form of competing power, authority, and dominion will be forever vanquished and demolished.

Some will claim that there is no reference here to a millennium or at least to time periods between these three resurrections. But they are most assuredly there. They are indicated by the two occurrences of the word *then*. The two Greek words used in the original (*epeita* and *eita*) are often found together; they imply a period of time between the poles specified. For example, we sing in the Thanksgiving hymn, "First the blade, and *then* the ear, / *Then* the full corn shall appear" (cf. Mark 4:28). These are the same *then*s as appear in 1 Corinthians 15. The wheat first must push its blade of new growth up above the soil; then it must be given time until it forms a head of grain; finally the full head bursts open on the top of the stalk. So it will be with the resurrections mentioned in 1 Corinthians 15. All humans will be raised by the power of God, but only in their assigned group and after the proper amount of time has elapsed (see fig. 2).

Thus far we have set the framework on which to locate

Figure 2 The Three Resurrections

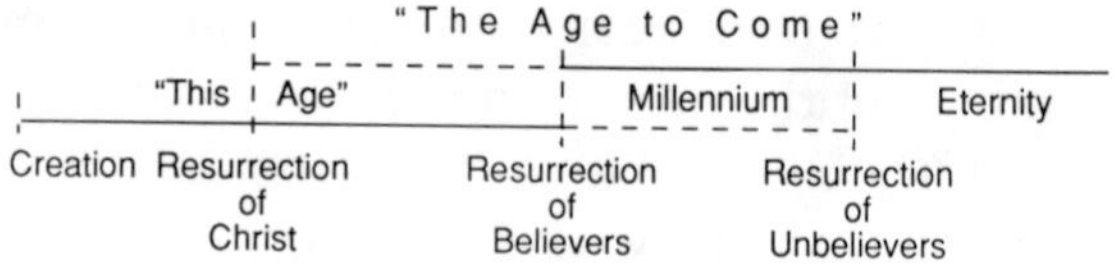

the key events in our Lord's consummation of time and history as we now know it. But how does all of this relate to the great schema of events and predictions in the Old and New Testaments? When is a passage referring to something that is totally future to us, and when can we say that we are enjoying part or all of what was prophesied?

The prophecies of Scripture must not be toyed with as if they can be made to say several things simultaneously or contradictory things. Nevertheless, many have felt that a prophet may have had multiple references in mind even if his sense was singlefold and constant. The phenomenon that we raise here is what is called prophetic foreshortening. Two or more events are predicted together even though they will be fulfilled separately. An excellent illustration of this temporal illusion is an observer who scans the distant horizon of two mountain peaks and comes to the preliminary conclusion that the two peaks must be side by side with little or no space between them since they appear to butt up against one another. Upon closer inspection, however, the mountains may prove to be ten to twenty miles apart.

In the area of prophecy the same phenomenon occurs. Willis J. Beecher spoke of generic predictions. In his definition "a generic prediction is one which regards an event as occurring in a series of parts, separated by intervals, and expresses itself in language that may apply indifferently to the nearest part, or to the remoter parts, or to the whole— in other words, a prediction which, in applying to the whole of a complex event, also applies to some of its parts."[1] The basic idea here is that some prophecies point ultimately to a final, climactic event, but that event is itself part of a series of events, all of which participate in and lead up to the climax. What holds this series together is not some type of double sense or deeper meaning which

1. Willis J. Beecher, *The Prophets and the Promise* (New York: Crowell, 1905; Grand Rapids: Baker, 1963), p. 130.

escaped the writer's purview, but rather a corporate or collective solidarity. That is, the whole set of events, such as
the long line of the Seed of the Messiah, makes up a collective totality and constitutes *only one idea*, even though
the events are spread over a large segment of history.

In the order of things, then, God gave a vision of the
future to his servants, the prophets. The prophets, in turn,
saw that vision in terms of both its near fulfilment(s) and
its climactic realization at the end of time. An analogy is
the sights of a gun barrel: the closer sight signifies near
and contemporary fulfilments, while the sight at the other
end of the gun barrel represents the ultimate event in the
messianic era. All of these fulfilments, and this is the most
important point, both near and distant, are so intimately
lined up when both sights are in focus that they make up
one sense or one meaning. The prophets were often un-
aware that in the same series there were a whole host of
other parts that had only begun to show up in their vision.
As a result of prophetic foreshortening, the prophet may
have seen only events A, B, and Z, and have had no idea
of what intervened. This view of generic prophecy was
espoused by the church at Antioch during the fifth, sixth,
and seventh centuries of the Christian Era.

Perhaps an illustration or two will be helpful in bringing
together what we have tried to teach concerning generic
predictions, prophetic foreshortening, and prophecies that
have a single meaning and collective or corporate solidarity. What we are trying to avoid is the popular but incor-
rect view that prophecy has a double sense or double
meaning to it. This is contrary to what the texts are actually claiming. It is also hurtful to a high view of Scripture, which includes the doctrine of inerrancy.

Malachi 4:5–6 promises that Elijah the prophet will return before the great and dreadful day of the Lord comes.
The scribes interpreted this text as meaning that Elijah
had to come before Messiah (Matt. 17:10–13; Mark
9:11–13). When asked about the matter by the disciples,
Jesus responded, "Elijah has come." He said it in such a

way that the disciples knew that he meant that John the Baptist was Elijah. Not only did our Lord affirm this shortly after the transfiguration, but he had bluntly said on another occasion, "He is the Elijah who was to come" (Matt. 11:14). Yet John forthrightly denied that he was the Christ, the Mosaic Prophet, or Elijah (John 1:21, 25). So was he or wasn't he Elijah?

John clearly was the messenger who would prepare the way for the Messiah, but that had been set forth in Isaiah 40:3–5 and Malachi 3:1. He was also a fulfilment of Malachi 4:5–6 in that he came "in the spirit and power of Elijah" (Luke 1:17). However, Elijah the Tishbite will himself return at the end of time, as Revelation 11 predicts, to minister once again.

So, then, there are near and distant aspects to the prediction of Malachi 4:5–6. But since all its parts and fulfilments are so organically related and share a collective wholeness, the sense of the prophecy is singular, not double or multiple. This is why Jesus taught that Elijah has already come and must still come to restore all things (Matt. 17:11–12). It is a matter of understanding the mindset. Some things were so interconnected that our Lord kept his ancient word alive for each generation by bringing into fruition new fulfilments of a series which ever looked forward to its ultimate enactment.

Joel's promise of the day of the Lord (Joel 2:28–32) is another example. When Peter stood up in front of the crowd on the day of Pentecost and affirmed, "This is what was spoken by the prophet Joel" (Acts 2:16), it appeared that there was no more to be said. The prophecy had been fulfilled! Yet all interpreters know that Pentecost took care of only the first two verses in that prophecy, and that only to an initial degree. Where were the "wonders in the heavens and on the earth, blood and fire and billows of smoke"? "The sun will be turned to darkness," promised Joel, "and the moon to blood."

These events yet await the consummation of history. The Book of Revelation picks up the same themes and projects them into the last days of earth's history. So once again we have a prophecy with a single meaning but near and distant fulfilments.

One could point to many other prophecies of the same type. John warns that the Antichrist is coming in the last hour of history, but already "many antichrists have come" (1 John 2:18). Just as there was a line of Davidic sons who passed on the promise until Messiah came, so there is an antimessianic line of power grabbers who are the contemporary holders of the title of Antichrist, possessing many of his sinister powers, until *the* Antichrist finally arrives on the scene.

Thus the near fulfilments are only harbingers or foretastes of the great climactic person or event that is to come in the end time. These events or persons—past, present, and future—make up one generic whole, the totality of the vision given to the prophet.

These, then, are some of the basic plays of the game of eschatology or, more simply, of the doctrine of last things. They will not prove to be very complicated if we pay close attention to the text. In fact, we will be all the more encouraged by the fact that God has not only given his word, but has kept that word alive through a series of events that share much in common with each other, until the climactic event comes to pass.

For Further Study

Cullmann, Oscar. "The Significance of the New Testament Terminology for Time." In *Dimensions of Faith,* ed. William Kimmel and Geoffrey Clive, pp. 305–40. New York: Twayne, 1960.

Guhrt, Joachim. "Time." In *The New International Dictionary of New Testament Theology,* ed. Colin Brown, vol. 3, pp. 826–33. Grand Rapids: Zondervan, 1978.

Kaiser, Walter C., Jr. "The Prophetic Use of the Old Testament in the New." In *The Uses of the Old Testament in the New,* pp. 61–100. Chicago: Moody, 1985.

PART 3

Practical Theology

11

Don't Substitute Riddles for What God Has Made Plain

T he rules for interpreting prophecy are as native to our beings as is the very process of speaking and understanding. Since all humans are made in the image of God and endowed with the gift of speech, it is obvious that they began to observe the laws of their communicative natures and faculties long before anyone began to codify these rules into some type of a science. Therefore, when we are called upon to give our assent to a rule of interpretation which is not founded on the usages of known speech, we ought to decline to yield to that pressure just as surely as we would refuse to convert into a new rule some previously unattested grammatical oddity. Rules of interpretation foreign to general usage are as inconsistent with proper hermeneutics as poor grammatical usage is with the science of grammar.

This truth must be pressed when it comes to interpreting the Scriptures. Often the friends of the Bible seem to bring it into as much disrepute as do its enemies; at least that is the impression one gathers from listening to some of the Bible's friendly interpreters who suddenly introduce secondary, spiritual, hidden senses and meanings that have little or no relation to the natural sense of the passage. The discovery of occult (secret, hidden) or double senses has been especially prominent in interpreting prophecy. This persistence forces us to ask a series of questions.

1. *Do the prophecies given in Scripture depend on a double meaning?* We speak of a double meaning when a text sets forth two senses which have little or no relation one to the other. We do not have in mind here what in the previous chapter we called generic prophecies, in which both the earlier partial fulfilment and the final complete fulfilment were in view from the outset, the one springing or germinating from the other. Rather, what we have in mind are passages which, though they have a clear meaning in themselves, a meaning plainly realized in the original Old Testament application of the passage, are alleged to have another sense and meaning pertaining to some other distinct subject. Here is where the problem arises.

Such a scheme of double senses forsakes and sets aside the common laws of language. Only when it is the intention to deceive or to tease another person by means of enigmas, double entendres, and the like, do we use double sense. Those who resort to ambiguity in prophetic language are either soothsayers who wish to conceal their uncertainties and consequently provide for differing outcomes, or charlatans who have no clear idea of what they are intending to communicate.

I am aware of the usual response to this charge: "The Bible is a *divine* book, and surely God has the right to hide some of his secrets in the plain words of Scripture, reserving them for times and persons of his choosing to unlock their mysteries." However, a revelation must be intelligible, or it is no revelation at all. As Moses Stuart has observed:

> The moment we assume that there is in Scripture a substantial departure from the *usus loquendi* [ordinary spoken sense], either in the choice of words, the construction

of sentences, or the modes of interpretation, that moment we decide, that so far as this departure extends, they are no revelation. . . . Did ever a considerate father undertake to teach his children, and yet employ language the words and exegetical principles of which were entirely beyond their cognizance? And when God speaks to his erring children, with an intention to enlighten and instruct them, and to reclaim them from their wandering ways, does he employ words in such a manner that no analogy drawn from human methods of interpreting language can enable men to understand what he communicates? . . . We must, therefore, either concede that the *usual* laws of language are to be applied to the Bible, or else that it is, and can be, no proper revelation to men, unless they are also to be inspired in order to understand it.[1]

Even though the Bible is a divine book, it still must be intelligible in order to be useful. And if it is intelligible, the use and meaning of words must conform to the ordinary spoken sense.

If it be objected that "the man without the Spirit does not accept the things that come from the Spirit of God" (1 Cor. 2:14), we will agree. The point, however, is not that there are two separate logics in the world, and that only those who have had some type of authentic religious experience with the Lord can understand the Bible. Paul's point is not about our intellectual ability, but about the nonspiritual person's refusal to welcome into his own life what he does know from reading the Scripture. That person is forever cut off from personally experiencing the things that come from the Spirit of God. But all of this is miles away from establishing that there is an occult, secret, or double sense to passages of Scripture.

2. *Even if there were a double sense, how could that double meaning be identified?* Who or what will arbitrate among the various meanings suggested and decide which

1. Moses Stuart, *Hints on the Interpretation of Prophecy*, 2d ed. (Andover, Mass.: Allen Morrill & Wardwell, 1842), pp. 15–17.

are to be accepted as authoritative and which are spurious? Short of saying that every person's fancy is his or her own rule, there does not appear to be any final court of appeal. Surely appeal cannot be made to the text itself, for it is not operating according to the normal rules if it has occult or hidden senses in it.

3. *What boundaries, then, are to be placed on the alleged double meanings?* Shall we allow every suggestion of a hidden or double sense to stand? Admit once that Scripture has a double or a mystic second sense, and the liberty of foisting the same on any passage of Scripture must be conceded to every reader of the text. It will do no good to complain that some are excessive and outlandish in the fantasies that they attempt to attach to given texts. Once the cow is out of the barn, there is no point in closing the door. There simply are no justifiable criteria for setting boundaries once the interpreter departs from the normal usage of language.

Usually the response is that "the abuse of a thing is no good argument against the use of it." But where the use is all abuse, that is not a valid complaint. A mystical secondary sense flies right in the face of all rules of communication and language. It is the advocates of this occult system who have the burden of proof on their shoulders to set the limits to which such a system can go. If there is a double sense to prophecy, then why not three, eight, fifteen, a hundred senses, all possessing the same degree of authority and authenticity—especially since there is no fixed tribunal before which any of these meanings must or can stand?

4. *What prevents interpreters from assigning an infinite number of meanings to prophecy?* To respond that normally an infinite number of meanings are not assigned would be to return to usage and to *usus loquendi* as the basis for assigning meaning to Scripture. That point belongs to our side, not to those advocating a mystical sense to Scripture.

There seems to be no limit for those who depart from the patterns of usage observed in language. The only nagging thought will be that every multiple explication of a text is simply the construction of the interpreter's own mind. It is thoroughly subjective.

5. *Can the double-meaning method of interpreting prophecy be used to establish doctrine?* Most advocates of the double-meaning system will hesitate to depend on it for setting out a doctrine for the church. But why such reluctance all of a sudden if this method can be used for spiritual insight and for other benefits?

Does not the reluctance to use double meanings for this purpose indicate that doubt does exist about the method's overall usefulness? If it is doubtful for doctrine, why should it be used in any other manner? Our conceptions of God, salvation, heaven, hell, and the wrath to come must not be determined by human fancy, imagination, or ingenuity. Why, then, in the area of prophecy is such wide latitude permitted? To set aside the historical, literal, and natural meaning of a text as but a temporary purpose of God and to substitute a more imaginative and fanciful interpretation of Scripture is to ignore the basic rules of speaking and listening worked into our beings by the gift of the image of God.

6. *Is the double-meaning method of interpreting prophecy supported by the practice of the New Testament writers?* Many base the notion of a double sense on the use of certain Old Testament passages in the New Testament. It is all too easily assumed that in quoting these passages the New Testament writers set forth a mystical secondary sense completely unknown to the writers of the Old Testament.

But have the New Testament writers done what some have suspected them of doing? There are but two major ways in which Old Testament predictive texts are used in the New Testament: (1) the New Testament writer may simply have cited the familiar language of the Old Testa-

ment when the words were useful for saying what he
wanted to say—in such cases there was no appeal to the
authority or original meaning of the Old Testament text;
or (2) the New Testament writer may have had the same
meaning in mind as did the Old Testament writer, especially in places which defend the gospel by pointing out
that the events of Messiah and his times were actually
forecast by the Old Testament scribes centuries prior to
the unfolding of the life of Jesus. It is this second way that
concerns us in this chapter.

In favor of the view that many of the prophecies have
a double sense, it is argued that some of the predictions
have a double referent: (1) a near, temporal, "now" event,
and (2) a remote, eternal, "not yet" event. This tension
between the "now" and the "not yet" has led many interpreters to declare themselves in favor of the double-sense
theory of interpreting prophecy.

There is a certain amount of truth to the claim that
some of the Bible's prophecies do exhibit a real tension
between the now and the not yet, but that truth does not
establish the double-sense theory. Said Frederic Gardiner:

> A prophecy may relate to more than one thing, nay, it may
> relate both to temporal and spiritual things, and yet have
> one sense. . . . The solution of the difficulty, therefore, is
> to be found mainly in two things: (1) in the frequent char-
> acter of prophecy as looking forward not simply to a single
> event or person, but to a series in the same line or pro-
> gressive fulfilment, having therefore always the same sense,
> but with a manifold application; and (2) in the combination
> of type with prophecy, so that what is said of the type in
> its typical character becomes necessarily prophetic of the
> antitype.[2]

Just as an element of the law may have only one meaning, but exhibit manifold applications, so prophecy also

2. Frederic Gardiner, *The Old and New Testaments in Their Mutual Relations* (New York: James Pott, 1885), pp. 267, 271–72.

may have a single meaning but numerous applications. For example, our Lord appealed to Hosea 6:6, "For I desire mercy, not sacrifice," as his justification for eating with tax collectors and sinners (Matt. 9:10–13) and for the disciples' picking some heads of grain and eating them on the Sabbath (Matt. 12:1–2, 7). The principle remained the same (i.e., the sense was single and not plural), but was made to bear on different subjects. Thus, no matter where we turn, the one sense intended by the author, though it may be applied to a wide variety of problems, governs all the passages where his words are quoted. The plurality of applications must not be used as a lever against the one sense and meaning.

The New Testament writers could not have appealed to the Old Testament for their doctrine of the Messiah and his mission by inaugurating a whole new set of meanings for texts which had not yielded this payload so far. What impact would that have made on those Jewish minds that were trained in the Scriptures? It would have been as ridiculous as our trying to give new meanings to the Koran in order to prove a point which is not contained in the Koran, but which would help our cause greatly! No, the New Testament writers, when fairly judged, exhibit that they did not appeal to mystical devices (e.g., midrash, pesher, or allegory) in order to gain new christological interpretations.

7. *But cannot God, the real author of Scripture, include a second meaning which is unknown to the human writer?* This suggestion supposes that in the Scriptures God speaks to us through some language of the angels, a language different from what we are accustomed to handling.

But is this an accurate representation of the facts of the case? Did not God choose to speak to us through men and through their languages? To the Hebrews, God spoke in Hebrew; to the Greeks, he spoke in Greek. Why? In order that he might be understood.

If the argument, however, is that God meant part to be

understood and to be subject to the normal rules of exegesis, but another part to be exempt from these constraints, then we must ask who will show us where we
are to draw the line between the two parts. And if it is
further argued that the New Testament writers were given
a revelation enabling them to draw such a line of demarcation between the two, does this not assume that the
New Testament use of the Old Testament introduced a
secondary, mystical sense which was unknown to the Old
Testament writers (a view we have already discredited)?
Must we also assume, conceding momentarily the previous point for the sake of the argument, that the number
of Old Testament passages to which an occult or divine
meaning can be attached is exhausted by the list of passages actually quoted in the New Testament? Or is this
list merely suggestive, encouraging us to go on and search
out additional passages that have a deeper meaning? And
what limits shall we introduce in the event that we do so?

Another question is whether the New Testament ex-
hibits the same duality of meaning as is alleged for Old
Testament prophecy, with part of the meaning being ob-
tained through the regular methods of exegesis, and the
rest coming in some direct revelation of the Holy Spirit.
In this case, are we not missing an essential element,
namely, a parallel to the authoritative stance of the New
Testament writer's inspired insight into the older part of
the canon?

Of course, there are parts of Scripture which any interpreter must concede as being to some degree obscure, if
not totally incomprehensible to him or her. But this is not
to say that those same texts were dark and difficult for
those to whom they were originally addressed. It would
be a case of jumping to conclusions if we assumed that
everything that gives us difficulty was also a difficulty for
others and therefore signals a portion of the text which
God deliberately left a *hyponoia*, in an occult state, to be
deciphered at some later stage of history when the code

would be cracked or revealed to selected interpreters by the Holy Spirit. No, when God addressed humanity, he did so in order to instruct, to reprove, to comfort, and not to mystify and to confuse.

When God reveals the future, he does so in order to be understood. There is not one shred of evidence for the presence of a secondary, mystical, occult *hyponoia* lying in, around, or under the text. The burden of proof is upon those who claim that such secondary senses and meanings are present. We ask only that they clearly spell out the criteria for locating the presence of such phenomena in the text and then give us the tools that we will need for unlocking them. Until then, we must basically interpret prophetic texts the way we exegete other passages.

For Further Study

Gardiner, Frederic. "The Alleged 'Double Sense' of Scripture." In *The Old and New Testaments in Their Mutual Relations*, pp. 262–73. New York: James Pott, 1885.

Jeremiah, David. "The Principle of Double Fulfillment in Interpreting Prophecy." *Grace Journal* 13 (1972): 13–29. A survey of a number of authors, taking the opposite view from what is advocated in this chapter.

Kaiser, Walter C., Jr. "The Apologetic Use of the Old Testament in the New." In *The Uses of the Old Testament in the New*, pp. 15–57. Chicago: Moody, 1985.

Stuart, Moses. *Hints on the Interpretation of Prophecy*, 2d ed., pp. 7–47. Andover, Mass.: Allen Morrill & Wardwell, 1842. This old essay supplied the main line of argumentation used in this chapter.

12

Don't Underestimate the Intelligibility of the Text

$$B$$iblical prophecy was not meant to be a secret open only to some special inner circle or a bomb set to go off on some type of timed sequencing. It is first and foremost a revelation from God. To argue that God has attached to the language employed in the text a meaning which has not yet been developed is to erect a very strange theory of revelation, not to mention the problem of communication itself. This is equivalent to asserting that revelation is a disclosure and an unveiling, but it is entirely unintelligible. What kind of disclosure of truth is simultaneously a concealing and obfuscation of what has been made plain?

Words are signs of things. They designate the things that were in the writer's or speaker's mind. How, then, could the words of some prophecies simply exist as words designating either no definite things at all or the wrong set of things? This question has even more force when one considers what those signs would ultimately be used to portray.

Surely God, who has perfect knowledge of all things, could connect with language many ideas unknown and incomprehensible to us in our present state of imperfection. However, what God knows in and of himself is one thing; what he chooses to reveal is a wholly different thing. Few will contend, we trust, that our God chooses to reveal to us what we are incapable of knowing. Otherwise, how could we trust his wisdom, his graciousness, or even his desire to communicate with us? God speaks in order to be understood. This affirmation raises another series of questions for all who wish earnestly to study biblical prophecy.

1. *Does the inspiration of prophecy guarantee comprehensiveness on all topics it touches or merely adequacy?* Only God knows comprehensively. There is nothing in revelation which insists that God gives all the information on any subject he chooses to discuss. Neither is there any rule that human language put to divine use necessarily entails a certain amount of elasticity.

It is enough if the words fairly, truly, and adequately convey some real contribution to the subject on which they speak. There is no guarantee of comprehensiveness, which may well include matters like chronology. Whatever was not received or imparted by the biblical writers is simply not a matter of revelation either to them or to us. Are we to argue, then, that we in our uninspired state have grasped a meaning the inspired writers did not? Surely on those terms we transgress the boundaries of good judgment.

2. *Didn't the prophets write better than they knew?* The opinion is widely shared, but has never been textually demonstrated, that the prophets spoke much better than they knew or understood.

The classic passage to which almost everyone turns who believes this myth is 1 Peter 1:10–12. Indeed, the prophets are pictured as having made a diligent search, but it was not to understand what they themselves had spoken. The object of their diligent search was the time of Christ's sufferings and subsequent glories. Literally, Peter says that they tried to find out "at what [time] or what manner of time (*eis tina ē poion kairon*)" the things would take place which were the subject of revelation. Had the apostle wanted to say that the prophets were searching for the meaning of the things they had spoken, he would have used the Greek expression *eis tina kai poion kairon* (they were inquiring into "what things and what manner of time" the Spirit had predicted). The point is that the interrogative *tina* ("what?") goes with the word for time (*kairon*). Even on the suggested alternative reading, Moses Stuart cautions: "Nor, in such a case, could it be interpreted as signifying, that they made a search in order to know the meaning of *what they had uttered,* but merely [that they searched for more] knowledge respecting the *subjects* of which they had spoken."[1]

But as the text stands, nothing more is claimed than that the prophets sought to know "at what time" the messianic era would be ushered in. They were anxious, as we all are, to know the time and manner of the new days announced here.

In the meantime they were certain about the five things we mentioned earlier (p. 24). Their words were directly related to the gospel dispensation in which we are now living. And central to that message of the evangel was that Messiah would come to suffer and then be honored with appropriate glory, events relevant not only for the Old Testament Jews, but also for those who believe today.

But the argument does not stop here. Why, we are asked, did the prophet Daniel hear but not understand when he was given a revelation (Dan. 12:8)? We must keep in view what it was that Daniel did not understand. Was it the words he was speaking? Not at all! It was the words that the angel was speaking. In addition to this, the sealing of these words until the end of time (v. 9) is more a reference to their *certainty* than to any alleged enigmatic quality

---

1. Moses Stuart, *Hints on the Interpretation of Prophecy,* 2d ed. (Andover, Mass.: Allen Morrill & Wardwell, 1842), p. 55.

about them. Isaiah 8:16 uses a very similar expression to indicate that the Lord's words were certain and secure; they would take place.

It must also be observed that Daniel's question in verse 8 involved a different point: "What shall be the end of these things?" (KJV). Previously in verse 6 one of the angels had asked, "How long shall it be to the end of these wonders?" (KJV). Daniel, however, had asked another question: What would the state of affairs be at the close of the time, times, and a half? It was this question which received no response. Our Lord had no further revelation for Daniel or for us on that subject. Thus the sealing up of the prophecy pointed only to its certainty, not to hiddenness.

Daniel did have an adequate understanding of what was going on, however. So vivid was his apprehension of what was to happen that he "was overcome and lay sick for some days" (Dan. 8:27 RSV). Surely he had more than just a vague impression of what might happen. Daniel was not at all hazy on what was to come. He knew—and it made him ill!

Had Daniel been interested in the temporal question, he would have asked, "How long (*'ad-mātay*)?" as the angel did in verse 6. Instead, he asked, "What (*māh*) will be the state of things at the close of time, times, and a half?" Clearly, then, Daniel expressed no ignorance over what he wrote. He merely wanted to receive more information if he could.

3. *Is the meaning of a prophecy to be limited to the truth-intention of the human author?* Louis Berkhof answers sharply, "There is no truth in the assertion that the intent of the secondary authors, determined by the grammatico-historical method, always . . . represents in all its fulness the meaning of the Holy Spirit."[2] But such an affirmation places us right back in the discussion of some

2. Louis Berkhof, *Principles of Biblical Interpretation: Sacred Hermeneutics* (Grand Rapids: Baker, 1950), p. 60.

of the points made in the previous chapter. It attempts to make prophecy transcend the limitations of language in some uncharted way that no one is willing to define.

When pressed further, the advocates of the position that biblical prophecy exceeds the linguistic consciousnesses of the writers flee to the case of Caiaphas in John 11:49–52:

> And one of them, named Caiaphas, being the high priest that same year, said unto them, "Ye know nothing at all, nor consider that it is expedient for us, that one man should die for the people, and that the whole nation perish not." And this spake he not of himself: but being high priest that year, he prophesied that Jesus should die for that nation; and not for that nation only, but that also he should gather together in one the children of God that were scattered abroad. [KJV]

Why it is maintained that normative teaching could come from one who played such a dreadful part in the death of our Lord, I will never be able to understand! If Caiaphas was accurate in his assessment of his countrymen when he scoffed, "Ye know nothing at all," did he really know any better? His advice was based solely on political expediency: to have one individual's rights trampled would be preferable to having a whole nation lose its privileges under a nervous Roman occupation force.

But what about the editorial comment made by John that Caiaphas spoke "not of himself: but being high priest that year, he prophesied"? Is this an example of an unintentional prophecy? We do not think so at all. John sees some wonderful irony, not only in what Caiaphas said, but also in the fact that he happened to be high priest that very year. Caiaphas was being the cool, calculating, and politically shrewd activist; the text does not claim that there was anything compelling him or any supernatural enduement from above.

In fact, John introduces his comment on Caiaphas's bravado talk with a strong Greek word, *alla* ("but"). Thus a strong line of demarcation is set between what Caiaphas said and meant and the new use to which John is applying the high priest's words. John now speaks by the inspiration of God and thus offers normative theology. Caiaphas's truth-intention is to be sharply contrasted with the significance that John found by turning Caiaphas's words around on him and stating what he would have been surprised to hear. Therefore, we must conclude that John's use of the word *prophesied* with regard to Caiaphas's declaration is filled with dripping sarcasm, irony, and conscious exaggeration.

John corrected Caiaphas's parochial point of view and turned it into a statement about the universal implications of Jesus' death. This is evident from John's expanding Caiaphas's expression "for the people" (v. 50) to say that Jesus' death would be "for that [Jewish] nation" (v. 51) and for "the children of God that were scattered abroad" (v. 52). The politically expedient Caiaphas worried only about Rome's wrath on Palestine; John saw more than national existence as being on the line. Jesus must die in order to form all nations into one spiritual family.

One last point should be mentioned. Caiaphas did not speak "of himself," that is, he did not speak on his own authority. John uses this expression six times (John 5:19; 7:18; 11:51; 15:4; 16:13; 18:34). In three of these six passages, the expression clearly means to say something on one's own (7:18; 16:13; 18:34). This is the meaning in 11:51 as well. If this is so, then what John is asserting is that Caiaphas's bitter proverb had significance as a principle that extended beyond the political quandary Israel found themselves in with Rome. John focuses not on the *method* of Caiaphas's speaking (as if he gave an unintended prophecy), but on the *significance* which his words have for those who have the revelation of God. If Caiaphas had given a prophecy in the ordinary sense of the word, there would have been no need for John to have corrected, improved, and reaimed his words. The revelations given by the Holy Spirit do not need to be corrected or modified!

All the attempts to credit the prophets' words with some type of *hyponoia* (hidden, double, or multiple sense) either incorrectly make the prophets into mere automata and simple mechanical robots to whom unclear words were dictated, or make them into individuals who were temporarily mad, taking a brief leave of their senses in a state of unconsciousness. Both options cut straight across all that Scripture claims to the contrary. Paul "would rather speak five intelligible words to instruct others than ten thousand words in a tongue" (1 Cor. 14:19).

We conclude by asking this question: How can we subscribe to the idea that prophecy was unintelligible when it was first spoken? If the prophets were given a revelation and a disclosure from God, would not that unveiling have been adequate and fully able to communicate? If we deny that these writers did indeed understand what was disclosed to them, two conclusions follow: (1) there was no real revelation to them; and (2) if inspired men did not understand, surely we uninspired individuals cannot.

The only case that fits the biblical claim is that the writers wrote exactly as it was revealed to them and that they understood the meaning of their prophecies. Let us take the blazing torch of revelation and not only use it for the so-called contemporary applications of the word to those times, but view it in the wholeness in which the author who received it from God meant it to be understood for all times.

"The true and full sense of any Scripture is not manifold but one," advised the Westminster Confession of Faith (1.9). That single sense and meaning exists even when there is a connected series of prophecies with sequential periods of fulfilment. This is true because each of the installments is leading toward the person, event, or act that is to come at the climactic fulfilment. Willis J. Beecher has referred to this as a cumulative fulfilment, that is to

say, a promise may continue being fulfilled in one generation after another, each installment exhibiting one or more
aspects of what will come in the final day.[3] The general
principle of the prophecy is reapplied time and again as
the word moves relentlessly towards its final day of
completion.

Prophecy constitutes one of the most amazing parts of
the whole process of revelation. By discovering deeper and
more subtle senses than those found in the grammar and
syntax, or by laying later Scripture over the earlier revelations, some interpreters may attempt to exceed what has
been so clearly revealed. But there is no need for that.
When properly understood, the prophetic word has a power
and a majesty all its own. It can defend itself against all
trivialities: those on the left which attempt to evacuate its
supernatural origins and precise disclosures of events, and
those on the right which worry that the mere explanation
of what is there will not appear worthy of the dignity and
depth a message from the Lord ought to have. After all,
prophecy is the word of God as revealed and as written!

It is hoped that this small collection of *Hints for Interpreting Biblical Prophecy* will stir a healthy conversation
among all branches of Christendom. We need to discuss
openly some of these matters once again, for they involve
over 27 percent of God's revelation to all peoples on earth.
They also set our day into the perspective of our Lord's
great redemptive conclusion to history as we know it. We
act most foolishly if we dig in on some of these matters.
Even worse, we offend the revelatory efforts of our Lord if
we decide to abandon this field of study altogether since
so many have gone to such excess on many of these topics.

God's prophetic word was meant to be understood and
is fully intelligible. While it is more complex in its cu-

3. Willis J. Beecher, *The Prophets and the Promise* (New York: Crowell,
1905; Grand Rapids: Baker, 1963), p. 130.

mulative fulfilments than some expect, it is much more simple than is surmised by others who try to attach special rules to it beyond the normal usage of language. In spite of these extremes, God continues to move relentlessly towards the goal he set ages ago for his plan. What a joy to know even as much as we do know because of his care in revealing it to his servants the prophets and apostles.

For Further Study

Payne, J. Barton. "Single Fulfillment." In *Encyclopedia of Biblical Prophecy: The Complete Guide to Scriptural Predictions and Their Fulfillment*, pp. 121–39. New York: Harper and Row, 1973.

Stuart, Moses. *Hints on the Interpretation of Prophecy.* 2d ed., pp. 47–66. Andover, Mass.: Allen Morrill & Wardwell, 1842.

Scripture Index